Physician Credentialing and Peer Review Answer Book

The Aspen Health Law Center
Patricia Younger, J.D.
Cynthia Conner, LL.L
Kara Kinney Cartwright, J.D.

An Aspen Publication®
Aspen Publishers, Inc.
Gaithersburg, Maryland
1995

This publication is designed to provide accurate and authoritative information in regard to the Subject Matter covered. It is sold with the understanding that the publisher is not engaged in rendering legal, accounting, or other professional service. If legal advice or other expert assistance is required, the service of a competent professional person should be sought. *(From a Declaration of Principles jointly adopted by a Committee of the American Bar Association and a Committee of Publishers and Associations.)*

Library of Congress Cataloging-in-Publication Data

Younger, Patricia A.
Physician credentialing and peer review
answer book / Patricia Younger, Cynthia Conner, Kara Kinney Cartwright.
p. cm.
Includes bibliographical references and index.
ISBN 0-8342-0658-7
1. Physicians—United States—Evaluation. 2. Medical audit.
3. Hospitals—United States—Medical staff—Evaluation.
I. Conner, Cynthia. II. Cartwright, Kara Kinney. III. Title.
[DNLM: 1. Credentialing—United States—legislation.
2. Peer Review, Health Care—United States—legislation.
3. Physicians—United States—legislation.
W 32.5 AA1 y7p 1995]
RA399.A3Y68   1995
362. 1'72—dc20
DNLM/DLC
for Library of Congress
94-42876
CIP

Editorial Resources: Amy Myers-Payne

Library of Congress Catalog Card Number: 94-42876
ISBN: 0-8342-0658-7

Printed in the United States of America

1   2   3   4   5

Table of Contents _____

List of Questions _____

1—Introduction to Credentialing and Peer Review

2—Participants in the Credentialing Process

3—Criteria for Medical Staff Membership

4—Delineation of Clinical Privileges

5—The Credentialing Process

Preapplication

Initial Application

Verification

Evaluation

6—Termination, Suspension, or Restriction of Privileges

Investigation

Hearing

Legal Challenges

Confidentiality Issues—Discoverability and Admissibility

7—Special Issues for Managed Care Organizations

8—Clinical Practice Guidelines

Introduction _____

The *Physician Credentialing and Peer Review Answer Book* is designed for medical staff services professionals, professionals involved in credentialing in a managed care setting, physicians, health care attorneys, governing board members, and other health care professionals who need quick and authoritative answers on a broad spectrum of questions concerning credentialing and peer review. The *Answer Book* addresses the legal issues as well as the practical aspects of credentialing and peer review.

Credentialing and peer review are more important than ever in our changing health care environment. As participation in various managed care organizations and inclusion in integrated delivery systems becomes more and more vital for physicians to continue to practice medicine in this country, credentialing and peer review issues become more critical. Credentialing criteria, which may tend to exclude various physicians, will probably be subject to increasing challenge. As the various health care entities strive to attract and retain only the most qualified physicians, and impose ever more stringent requirements on those physicians, the peer review process will receive even greater emphasis than it has in the past.

The *Answer Book* is intended to be a handy reference which is comprehensive yet easily accessible. Although the book does address legal issues on both the state and federal levels, the reader should be aware that the law varies from state to state and that the law varies with time due to the enactment of new state statutes and regulations or due to new court decisions.

How To Use This Book _____

This *Answer Book* attempts to use simple language and avoid complex terminology when possible, although technical language that is necessary and appropriate to describe legal concepts may appear at various points in the book.

CITATIONS

Citations of authority are provided as research aids for those who need to pursue particular items in greater detail.

QUESTION NUMBERING

The question numbering system is simple, numbering questions consecutively within each chapter.

QUESTION LISTS

The List of Questions following the Table of Contents is a detailed listing of questions intended to help the reader locate areas of immediate interest. The Table of Contents at the beginning of the volume identifies the page on which each list of questions appears.

INDEX

At the back of the book is an index, provided as a further aid to locating specific information. All references in the index are to question numbers rather than page numbers.

ABBREVIATIONS

Due to the breadth of the subject area, various terms are either abbreviated or designated by acronyms throughout the book. Generally, the first time each such abbreviation is used, it follows the full term with which it is associated in the text.

1

Introduction to Credentialing and Peer Review

Q.1:1 What is credentialing?

Credentialing is the process of obtaining information, verifying the information, and evaluating applicants who want to obtain or renew medical staff membership and/or obtain, renew, or revise clinical privileges at health care facilities. Managed care organizations (MCOs), such as health maintenance organizations (HMOs) and preferred provider organizations (PPOs), also credential physicians who seek to become participating providers in the MCO. Large group practices, independent practice associations (IPAs), and some medical societies also perform credentialing.

Credentialing is generally performed at:

- initial appointment
- initial delineation and granting of clinical privileges
- reappointment and renewal or revision of clinical privileges

(Unless otherwise indicated, such as in the section on special issues for managed care organizations, the majority of the following discussion will refer to credentialing in a hospital setting.)

Q.1:2 What is peer review?

An essential part of ongoing evaluation in the credentialing process is peer review, which involves the review of a practitioner's clinical skills and professional conduct by a committee composed of the practitioner's peers.

Q.1:3 Who must be credentialed?

The credentialing process applies to all physicians and other independent practitioners (those permitted by law and by the individual hospital or MCO to provide patient care without direction or supervision, such as dentists and podiatrists) who seek or exercise clinical privileges regardless of whether they also seek or hold medical staff membership. The credentialing process should apply whether the individual is a contract practitioner, such as a member of a medical group that has an exclusive contract for emergency department services; a hospital-based physician employed by the facility; or an independent contractor. Even individuals seeking temporary privileges must be subject to the credentialing process.

Allied health practitioners, such as physician assistants and nurse practitioners, who cannot practice independently, are subject to a separate credentialing process delineated in the medical staff bylaws, rules, regulations, or policies. These practitioners are not considered medical staff members.

Q.1:4 Why do credentialing?

The first and foremost reason for performing credentialing is to ensure that patients receive quality medical care from qualified practitioners. The vast majority of medical staff members do not have credentialing problems. However, when there are problems, and they are not detected and appropriately addressed by the credentialing entity, the consequences as far as patient harm can be devastating.

The courts and legislatures have recognized that hospitals have a duty to the public to properly credential their medical staffs. Therefore, to minimize legal liability to patients for physician performance and to ensure compliance with state, federal, and local law, hospitals must ensure that credentialing procedures are properly carried out.

In addition, hospitals must meet certain credentialing standards set by the Joint Commission on Accreditation of Healthcare Organizations (Joint Commission) in order to be accredited by that organization. The Joint Commission accreditation may influence licensing and reimbursement matters (See **Q.1:6**, below) and create a public perception of high quality care.

In MCOs, credentialing is performed because of the same concern for quality patient care and limitation of liability. In addition, MCOs focus on the economic aspects of health care delivery to a greater degree than hospitals have in the past. Part of the credentialing process in MCOs includes an evaluation of whether the care is rendered in an effective and cost-effective manner.

Q.1:5 Is credentialing regulated by law?

Credentialing is affected by state and federal statutory law and regulations as well as by court decisions.

Q.1:6 How does state law address credentialing?

Some states have statutory provisions, often found in the hospital licensure laws, that explicitly indicate what criteria must or may be considered in making credentialing decisions. While such laws may be viewed initially as restrictive, they may contain language that can be interpreted broadly. In New York, for example, in addition to consideration of competence, character, and patient care concerns, the law permits consideration of "objectives of the institution." [N.Y. Public Health Law §2801-b] Florida law includes a laundry list of factors and concludes with "and by such other elements as may be determined by the governing board." [Fla. Stat. §395.011]

Hospitals must be licensed to operate and comply with the requirements contained in state licensure laws and regulations. Some state laws indicate that hospitals accredited by the Joint Commission are "deemed" to have met the requirements of the licensure law and are not subject to state inspection. Therefore, hospitals relying on the Joint Commission accreditation for licensure purposes must fulfill its requirements regarding credentialing.

Several states also have "any willing provider" laws that apply to MCOs. Such laws specify that MCOs cannot categorically exclude a particular class of providers, such as psychologists, podiatrists, or nurse midwives. The MCO, therefore, must consider such providers as potential participants in the MCO and evaluate each provider fairly. All candidates for participation, however, must be professionally qualified and meet other established criteria for participation before they will be accepted as MCO providers.

Most states also have what are known as peer review laws, which protect the confidentiality of peer review information and grant either qualified or absolute immunity to those who participate in the peer review process.

Q.1:7 What federal laws address credentialing?

Medicare Conditions of Participation, the Health Care Quality Improvement Act, and the Americans with Disabilities Act all address or affect the credentialing process.

Q.1:8 What are the Medicare Conditions of Participation?

To be reimbursed under both the Medicare and Medicaid programs, hospitals must comply with federal regulations called Conditions of Participation. These regulations set out the standards hospitals must meet in a variety of operational and strategic areas in order to participate in the Medicare program and thereby receive Medicare reimbursement. If a hospital meets Joint Commission standards, it is "deemed" to have met the Medicare Conditions of Participation. Joint Commission standards directly address credentialing issues. [42 C.F.R. §482.1]

Q.1:9 How do the Medicare Conditions of Participation affect credentialing?

The Conditions of Participation specifically address credentialing matters. They require that the governing body establish criteria for the selection of members of the medical staff. Staff members must have the appropriate character, competence, training, experience, and judgment. [42 C.F.R. §482.12(a)(6)] The medical staff is directed to conduct periodic appraisals of medical staff members. [42 C.F.R. §482.22(a)(1)]

Q.1:10 What is the Health Care Quality Improvement Act?

The Health Care Quality Improvement Act of 1986 (HCQIA) is a federal law that grants immunity to peer review activity and seeks to improve the quality of health care through reporting requirements. [P.L. 99-660] The act provides immunity under federal and state law for any individual or body that participates in the peer review process, including witnesses and providers of information.

Q.1:11 How does the HCQIA affect credentialing?

The HCQIA contains both reporting requirements and immunity provisions that affect credentialing. The law requires health care entities to report certain adverse actions taken against health care practitioners. Information must be requested from the National Practitioner Data Bank (NPDB) when practitioners apply for positions on the medical staff, clinical privileges at the hospital, or participation status in an HMO. Information also must be requested every two years at the time of reappointment of such individuals. (See **Q.5:3** for a more detailed explanation of the NPDB.)

The immunity provisions provide persons giving information to professional review bodies and those assisting in review activities limited immunity from damages that may arise as a result of adverse decisions that affect a physician's medical staff privileges. The immunity provisions apply only if certain procedural safeguards are satisfied. (See **Q.6:24** for a more detailed explanation of these procedural safeguards.)

If the procedural and reporting requirements of the act are met, members of a professional review body will not be liable in damages under any law, except the Civil Rights Act or the Clayton Act, which is an antitrust law.

Q.1:12 What is the Americans with Disabilities Act?

The *Americans with Disabilities Act* (ADA) is a federal law that prohibits discrimination against individuals with disabilities in private employment, public services and transportation, public accommodations, and telecommunications services.

Title I of the ADA states that "no covered entity shall discriminate against a qualified individual with a disability because of the disability of such individual in regard to job application procedures, the hiring, advancement, or discharge of employees, employee compensation, job training, and other terms, conditions, and privileges of employment." [42 U.S.C. §12112(a)] Physicians who are employed by the hospital are covered under Title I, but it is not clear whether independent contractors who are members of the medical staff are covered as well. Because medical staff members have been considered "employees" entitled to the protection of Title VII of the Civil Rights Act, there is a possibility that they may be considered employees under Title I.

Title II of the ADA prohibits discrimination on the basis of disability by a public entity, including the granting of licenses or certificates.

Title III of the ADA prohibits any private entity that owns, leases, or operates a place of public accommodation from discriminating against an individual on the basis of disability. "Public accommodation" is broadly defined and includes most privately owned businesses that serve the public. Both hospitals and the professional offices of health care providers fall within this definition and must, therefore, make their facilities accessible to disabled practitioners.

Q.1:13 What employers are subject to the ADA?

The ADA applies to employers who employ 25 or more employees as of July 26, 1992 and to employers who employ 15 or more employees as of July 26, 1994. [42 U.S.C. §12111 (5)]

Q.1:14 What is considered a disability under the ADA?

A disability is defined as

- a physical or mental impairment that substantially limits one or more of the major life activities,
- a record of such an impairment, or
- being regarded as having such an impairment. [42 U.S.C. §12102 (2)]

Q.1:15 What is a physical or mental impairment under the ADA?

Under the ADA, physical or mental impairment is defined as:

- any physiological disorder, condition, cosmetic disfigurement, or anatomical loss affecting one or more specified body systems: neurological, musculoskeletal, special sense organ, respiratory (including speech organs), cardiovascular, reproductive, digestive, genitourinary, hemic and lymphatic, skin, and endocrine systems, or
- any mental or psychological disorder, such as mental retardation, organic brain syndrome, emotional or mental illness, and specific learning disabilities. [EEOC Reg. §1630.2(h)]

Q.1:16 What are the definitions of "major life activities" and "substantially limits" under the ADA?

"Major life activities" include caring for oneself, performing manual tasks, walking, seeing, hearing, speaking, breathing, learning, and working. [EEOC Reg. §1630.2 (i)]

"Substantially limits" means that a person cannot perform a major life activity that can be performed by the average person in the general population, or he or she is significantly restricted as to the condition, manner, or duration in which he or she can perform a major life activity compared to the average person in the general population.

For the major life activity of "working," "substantially limited" means significantly restricted in the ability to perform within a class of jobs or within a broad range of jobs in various classes as compared to the average person having comparable training, skills, and abilities. [EEOC Reg. §1630.2(j)(3)(ii)]

Q.1:17 What is a qualified individual with a disability?

A qualified individual with a disability is one who has the skills, experience, education, and other job-related requirements of the position. A qualified individual can perform the essential functions of the job with or without reasonable accommodation.

Q.1:18 How does the ADA affect credentialing?

Under the ADA, the pre-employment process cannot discriminate against qualified persons with disabilities. Therefore, whether the physician is seeking employee or participation status in an HMO or is applying for clinical privileges, preapplication forms as well as application forms must be worded carefully to avoid eliciting information regarding disabilities. (See **Q.5:15**)

The ADA indicates that an employer cannot require a medical examination as a condition of employment. An employer can require a medical examination after a job offer has been made, however, if all persons within the job category are required to undergo medical examinations. The medical examination does not have to be job-related, but if information is used to screen out a disabled person, it must be job-related. For example, a hospital could require all surgeons to undergo eye exams. If a surgeon is severely visually impaired, the hospital could screen that surgeon out because good vision is necessary to effectively perform surgery. On the other hand, while all physicians could conceivably be required to undergo eye examinations, a poor result could not be used to screen out psychiatrists, as good vision is not job-related for that specialty.

Medical examination information must be kept confidential and must be kept in files separate from the routine employment files.

Q.1:19 Can a hospital require physicians to undergo a pre-employment drug test as part of the process of assessing physical and mental condition?

While the ADA prohibits pre-employment medical inquiries and examinations, testing for the illegal use of drugs is not considered a medical examination. [42 U.S.C. §12114]

Further, the ADA does not protect illegal drug users, defined as individuals who are either using illegal drugs or illegally using prescription drugs that are controlled substances. [42 U.S.C. §12114, 29 C.F.R. §1630.3] Thus, testing for illegal drugs or for the illegal use of controlled substances prior to making an offer of employment does not violate the law. An employer may reject an applicant who tests positive for illegal drugs.

The situation is more complicated, however, if an employer conducts pre-employment screening for commonly abused prescription drugs. Because the legal use of such drugs is protected under the ADA, an employer would have to determine whether the applicant's use of the drug is in accordance with a lawful prescription before refusing to hire the individual. According to the latest EEOC guidance, if an applicant tests positive for illegal drug use, the employer may validate the test results by asking the applicant about lawful drug use that may have resulted in a positive drug result. If an employer tests solely for unlawful drug use but receives test results indicating lawful drug use, the employer has not violated the ADA. [EEOC: Enforcement Guidance on Pre-Employment Inquiries Under the Americans with Disabilities Act, May 19, 1994]

Because drug testing is fraught with risk management issues as well as operational issues, before an employer implements a drug testing program, the employer should consult with an attorney with expertise in employment and health care law.

Q.1:20 How have the courts addressed the question of hospital responsibility for the credentialing process?

Beginning with the *Darling* case in 1965, the courts have established clearly that hospitals have a direct responsibility for the quality of care provided by independent medical staff members. Failure to meet that responsibility is referred to as corporate negligence. To fulfill its corporate duty, a hospital must carefully select the physicians it permits to practice medicine at the facility and must monitor the care they provide.

The following cases are illustrative of court rulings on this issue:

- *Darling v. Charleston Community Mem. Hosp.*, 211 N.E.2d 253 (Ill. 1965) *cert. denied*, 383 U.S. 946 (1966).

This was the first case to hold that hospitals have a corporate duty to monitor the patient care being provided in the facility. The actual decision was somewhat limited. Hospitals have a duty to see that employees observe the condition of patients and report their findings. If the attending physician does not do what is clearly proper, the employees are to report to higher authority so that a consultation can be arranged. The philosophy underlying the decision, however, has had far-reaching implications. A number of subsequent opinions have looked back to *Darling* in finding an institutional duty to monitor the performance of medical staff members.

- *Mitchell County Hosp. Auth. v. Joiner*, 189 S.E.2d 412 (Ga. 1972).

In this case involving the delegation of review to the medical staff, the hospital governing body argued that it could have no liability for the inadequate performance of a medical staff member since the practitioner was licensed and his appointment had been recommended by the medical staff. The court disagreed, holding that the governing body's delegation of authority to the medical staff to screen applicants could not relieve the institution of liability. The medical staff was acting as agent of the governing body, and whether the latter knew or should have known of the practitioner's incompetence was a question of fact to be determined by a jury.

- *Purcell v. Zimbelman*, 500 P.2d 335 (Ariz. App. 1972).

The Arizona appeals court addressed the question of institutional responsibility to monitor medical staff performance. It stated that a hospital could not escape liability simply because it had fulfilled its duty to establish a review mechanism if its Department of Surgery (to which review had been delegated and which was acting for and on behalf of the governing body) negligently failed to take action against a surgeon whose lack of skill should have been apparent.

- *Johnson v. Misericordia Community Hosp.* 294 N.W.2d 501 (Wis. App. 1980), *aff'd.* 301 N.W.2d 156 (Wis. 1981).

Wisconsin's highest court strongly affirmed that a hospital has a legal duty to properly review a physician's credentials upon application to the medical staff, finding a hospital liable for injuries caused by an unqualified physician who had negligently been granted orthopedic privileges. The court ruled that the hospital had contributed to the patient's injury simply by allowing the physician to have staff privileges.

- *Elam v. College Park Hosp.*, 183 Cal. Rptr. 156 (Cal. App. 1982).

This case reaffirmed a hospital's duty to both select and review staff physicians adequately. The court held that a hospital that fails to perform this duty satisfactorily may be liable for the malpractice of physicians who are neither employees nor agents of the hospital.

Q.1:21 What other sources guide the credentialing process?

The Joint Commission has several standards relating to the credentialing process, found mostly in the medical staff standards, although a few pertinent standards are found in the governing body standards. Facilities that are accredited by the Joint Commission must follow the credentialing requirements set out in these standards.

The National Committee for Quality Assurance (NCQA) has established voluntary standards to assess managed care organizations. (See **Q.7:6** for an in-depth discussion of those standards.)

Q.1:22 What are the usual categories of medical staff membership?

Most hospital bylaws provide for various categories of medical staff appointments, which may be classified as full or limited.

Full appointment refers to "active" medical staff. The appointee is entitled to full participation in medical staff government. Members of this staff are responsible for all major organizational and administrative duties that are performed by the medical staff. Active staff members are accorded the privileges of voting and holding office. In the average hospital, the majority of medical staff appointments are to the active medical staff.

Limited appointment categories include *associate* or *provisional, courtesy, consulting,* and *honorary* or *emeritus* medical staff. Most hospitals create an *associate,* sometimes termed *provisional* staff, consisting of those practitioners who are relatively new to the staff (generally in their first 12 months, or whatever time period is indicated in the medical staff bylaws) and who are under consideration for advancement to the active staff. Members of the associate staff are customarily appointed and assigned to departments in the same manner as are active staff members. Although they may not hold office, they may be required to serve on certain medical staff and hospital committees. They may or may not have voting privileges, and appointment is usually probationary in nature. Members of the associate staff may be subject to proctoring so that there can be an evaluation of the physician's clinical competence in addition to the paper credentials. Associate staff members may have clinical privileges equal to those granted to members of the active staff.

The *courtesy* medical staff, if a hospital chooses to have one, is composed of those practitioners who are otherwise eligible for active staff membership but do not normally admit a large number of patients. Their hospital practice is confined, by choice or by medical staff decision, to consultation, although an occasional patient may be admitted. Members of the courtesy staff ordinarily are not granted the right to vote or to hold office. Depending on the needs of the institution, they may be excused from emergency department service or other duties required of active and associate staff members. Members of the courtesy staff are usually not seeking advancement to the active staff and may be required to have active staff membership at other hospitals.

In addition to or in place of a courtesy staff, the hospital may also establish a *consulting* medical staff composed of practitioners of recognized professional ability who serve only as consultants and who do not admit patients. Consulting staff normally may neither vote nor hold office, nor are they members of any other category of the medical staff.

The *honorary* medical staff is reserved for practitioners whom the hospital wishes to honor. The appointment, also called *emeritus*, recognizes former staff members, retired physicians, or other practitioners of outstanding reputation. Members of this category do not vote or hold office and ordinarily do not admit patients. If they do, they must be evaluated as any other practitioner with staff privileges.

Q.1:23 Why is membership category important when discussing credentialing?

When an applicant seeks medical staff membership, he or she applies for a specific category of membership, each of which entails different responsibilities and permits the exercise of different rights. The delineation of clinical privileges must be appropriate for the category to which the physician belongs.

Q.1:24 Do physicians or other practitioners have a right to obtain medical staff membership or clinical privileges?

Health care practitioners do not have a right to obtain medical staff membership or clinical privileges. The U.S. Supreme Court affirmed this in *Hayman v. Galveston*, 273 U.S. 414 (1927). However, they do have a right to fair and equal treatment in the consideration of their application for membership and privileges. Applicants must meet all legal requirements and all of the established criteria of a particular facility before they will be granted membership or privileges.

In addition, the courts have recognized that health care facilities can make business decisions that may limit a practitioner's access to a facility. The vast majority of case law, for example, affirms the rights of hospitals to enter into exclusive contracts for the provision of particular services as long as the decision is related to legitimate business reasons. Such contracts necessarily restrict physician access to certain privileges.

Q.1:25 What is medical staff membership?

Appointment to the medical staff and clinical privileging are distinct. There are specific requirements an applicant must meet in order to be granted staff membership, such as licensure, professional liability coverage, DEA (Drug Enforcement Administration) number, physical and mental health, and ability to work with others. Generally, as a condition of appointment to the staff, the practitioner must assume certain duties and responsibilities, such as serving on various medical staff committees.

Q.1:26 What are clinical privileges?

Clinical privileges represent specific procedures or groups of procedures that the hospital governing body authorizes a practitioner to perform. The Joint Commission defines clinical privileges as "permission to provide medical or other patient care services in the granting institution, within well-defined limits, based on the individual's professional license and his/her experience, competence, ability, and judgment." [MS 1 (1994)] (See Chapter 4 for an expanded discussion of clinical privileges.)

Q.1:27 Can individuals hold clinical privileges and not be members of the medical staff?

Yes, individuals can hold clinical privileges without being a medical staff member. The Joint Commission states that all individuals who are permitted by law and by the hospital to provide patient care services independently in the hospital must have delineated clinical privileges whether or not they are members of the medical staff. [MS 2.2 (1994)] Physicians who are granted temporary privileges are not members of the medical staff. (See **Q.4:13** regarding temporary privileges.) A proviso is that individuals granted the privilege to admit patients to inpatient services must be members of the medical staff. [MS 2.16.1 (1994)]

Q.1:28 Does the medical staff comprise only physicians?

The majority of the medical staff comprises physicians. However, other independent practitioners may also be medical staff members, depending on state law and the bylaws of the individual facility. Some state laws require, for example, that dentists be eligible for staff membership.

Q.1:29 Can the hospital decide to limit the size of the medical staff or accept only certain types of physicians?

A hospital may make a business decision that it will not accept further applicants for medical staff membership or privileges. This decision is generally made on the basis of a medical staff development plan. The hospital may close the entire medical staff or, what is more likely, close certain departments or services. This decision should be made by the governing body after consideration of the needs of the community and the capabilities of the hospital. There should be substantial input from the hospital administration in creating a medical staff development plan that supports a closed medical staff. The business purpose should be reasonable and fully documented.

The New Jersey Supreme Court held that adoption of a closed-staff policy as a solution to bed overcrowding and overuse of hospital resources is reasonable. [*Desai v. St. Barnabas Medical Center*, 510 A.2d 662 (N.J. 1986)] However, it found that an exception to the policy that allowed the hospital to grant staff privileges to physicians who were already associated with current medical staff had a discriminatory impact on those physicians and their patients in the community who were not associated with the hospital's medical staff and that it was invalid.

The court held that if a hospital policy decision serves an evident public health purpose, it will be sustained even if it has a restrictive effect. If it cannot be shown, however, that a restrictive staff admissions policy reasonably furthers a legitimate health care objective, then the policy is discriminatory and, therefore, invalid.

In essence, the granting of an exclusive contract is a method of creating a closed department. The case law overwhelmingly upholds the validity of exclusive contracts, which have often been challenged on antitrust grounds.

Q.1:30 How are health care providers other than members of the medical staff evaluated?

Allied health professionals, such as certified registered nurse anesthetists, physician assistants, and nurse midwives, are considered "dependent" practitioners in that they are subject to some degree of supervision. The medical staff has a responsibility to ensure the qualifications and competence of allied health professionals. Some term this "credentialing" in the broad sense. Allied health professionals are granted privileges or the authority to provide specific patient services. The procedures for appointment and scope of practice should be set out in the medical staff rules and regulations. These individuals are subject to evaluation through the quality assurance and utilization review processes.

All health care providers who participate in the delivery of health care services to patients must be evaluated for competence. In most cases, this evaluation is done through the regular employment process and periodic evaluation by a supervisor. The typical employment process, for example, will reveal whether a laboratory technician has received the proper training and certification necessary to be employed for a particular position in the hospital laboratory and will include contacting previous employers as part of an investigation into the individual's competence.

Q.1:31 Are medical residents subject to the same credentialing, appointment, and clinical privileging procedures?

The Accreditation Council for Graduate Medical Education (ACGME) has established graduate medical education requirements that govern the training of residents. Residents are not appointed as members of the medical staff. The Joint Commission indicates that because "house staff" practice under clinical supervision, they do not need to be given clinical privileges, although they must have evaluations and position descriptions. [*Medical Staff Credentialing: Questions and Answers About the Joint Commission's Standards*, The Joint Commission on Accreditation of Healthcare Organizations. Oakbrook, IL, 1993, 31]

Q.1:32 What are the credentialing issues if a military physician "moonlights" at a civilian facility?

Military physicians can moonlight in a civilian facility with the approval of the commanding officer of the military treatment facility. It should be noted that while the military conducts its own extensive credentialing process, physicians serving on active duty are not required to be licensed in each state in which they serve. Therefore, a facility considering granting privileges to a military physician should specifically inquire about state licensure. In addition, active-duty physicians do not usually carry their own medical malpractice insurance, so this is another area that should be queried.

Q.1:33 Who can be sued for negligent credentialing?

Hospitals, medical staffs, and individual participants in the credentialing process may be sued for negligent credentialing. There is substantial case law on the issue of credentialing. (See **Q.1:20,** which sets out a number of cases that illustrate hospital liability for negligent credentialing.) In addition to finding hospitals liable for negligent credentialing, several cases have held that the medical staff, as an entity, may be sued. [See *Bell v. Sharp Cabrillo Hosp.*, 260 Cal. Rptr. 886 (Cal. App. 1989).] Individual members of the credentials committee may also be sued. For example, a physician contesting a credentialing decision may allege that members of the committee conspired against him or her in violation of the antitrust laws.

Q.1:34 What protections are available for members of the credentials committee?

There are several protections available for the members of the credentials committee. The hospital's insurance should cover the expense of litigation. State law may offer qualified or absolute immunity for participation in peer review activities. The first place to look for such immunity is in the state peer review law whether that law is incorporated into the hospital licensing law, the state evidentiary code, or elsewhere. Other sources of state law should not be overlooked. For example, the state Medical Practice Act, Medical Studies Act, or Not-for-Profit Corporations Act may contain immunity provisions for peer review activity. In addition to state law, federal law may offer some protection. If the due process procedures specified in HCQIA are followed, peer review participants also enjoy immunity from suit under that law.

Q.1:35 What other grounds for suit might arise from the credentialing/peer review process?

A disgruntled practitioner may level charges of defamation; interference with contract or prospective business relations; discrimination on the basis of race, color, religion, sex, disability, or national origin; or antitrust violations.

Q.1:36 What is defamation?

Defamation is defined as holding up a person to ridicule, scorn, or contempt in a respectable and considerable part of the community.

Defamation includes both libel and slander. Slander consists of spoken statements injurious to reputation, while libel is defamation preserved in a more permanent form than the spoken word. It is usually written but may also take the form of recordings, film, photographs, and the like. Any defamatory material that is not communicated to third parties is not actionable because of the lack of publication.

Both forms of defamation are possible in the context of medical staff review procedures. Statements about a practitioner may be made in hospital committee meetings, and the preparation of written reports and references evaluating physicians is a routine practice in most hospitals.

Q.1:37 What are defenses to defamation?

Truth: The most basic defense to a charge of defamation is that the statements complained of are the truth. If their truth can be demonstrated, it is unlikely that the plaintiff will prevail; in fact, it is unlikely that a suit ever would be brought in the first place.

If the statements cannot be shown by competent evidence to be true, they still might not be grounds for a finding of liability depending on the circumstances under which they were made. In one case, for example, a physician who wrote a letter to a hospital credentials committee and hospital officials criticizing another physician was found not liable for defamation because the physician had a reasonable basis for believing the truth of the statements in the letter. [*Guntheroth v. Rodaway*, 727 P.2d 982 (Wash. 1986)] In another case, an Illinois court found that a hospital's statements to the press regarding the termination of a physician's medical staff privileges were protected by qualified privilege. It further held that the hospital's statements about the matter in a staff memo were expressions of opinion, not actionable defamation. [*Rodriguez-Erdman v. Ravenswood Hospital Medical Center*, 545 N.E.2d 979 (Ill. Ct. App. 1989)]

In a credentialing context, the Seventh Circuit ruled that a physician cannot recover for defamation when a hospital administrator makes statements in response to inquiries from other hospitals unless the physician can show that the administrator's comments caused potential employers to deny his application for staff privileges. In that case, a physician voluntarily resigned from a hospital following allegations of sexual harassment and Medicaid fraud. The physician then applied for staff privileges at a second hospital, whose administrator began to check the physician's references. Five references indicated that the physician was medically competent but unable to get along with others. An administrator from the hospital from which the physician had resigned told the potential employer that the physician had resigned "under the direction of the hospital attorney," had been indicted for Medicaid theft, and had sexually assaulted a nurse. After the physician's application for privileges at the second hospital was denied, he sued the first hospital. The trial court found that the administrator's comment regarding sexual misconduct was true and, therefore, privileged under the Indiana peer review statute. However, the court found the comments regarding the Medicaid indictment and resignation under the direction of the hospital attorney were incomplete, misleading, and malicious, and, therefore, not protected. The trial court nonetheless ruled against the physician, finding that the administrator's remarks had not caused the second hospital to deny his application. The physician appealed. [*Walton v. Jennings Community Hospital*, 999 F.2d 277 (7th Cir. 1993)]

The Seventh Circuit upheld the trial court's ruling that the administrator's comments were not the proximate cause of the second hospital's decision to deny the application. Acknowledging that an event can have more than one proximate cause, the court nonetheless ruled that the trial court's finding was valid. The individual at the second hospital who decided not to grant privileges to the physician testified that the comments played no part in his decision and that his decision was based on the physician's inability to get along with other physicians. Because the trial court found that testimony credible, the comments could not have caused the denial under any causation standard, the appeals court concluded.

Consent: If the practitioner about whom otherwise defamatory statements are made has consented to their being made, no cause of action in defamation is possible.

The hospital bylaws may be used as a vehicle to protect against liability for defamation. The applicant for medical staff appointment may be required to consent to the communication of all information as a condition of consideration of his or her application for appointment. A statement contained in the bylaws that the applicant agrees that all communications relative to review of the practitioner's performance and qualifications shall enjoy a privilege against claims of defamation may be persuasive to the court in finding the applicant to have consented to the making of the statements. It is also persuasive to include the statement on the application itself, and the application is signed by the physician.

In a Michigan case, a physician whose surgical privileges were restricted wrote to the credentials committee of the hospital requesting that the specific reasons for the action be stated. At the request of the credentials committee, the chairperson of the Department of Surgery wrote a letter to the committee listing 13 instances of inadequate performance and unprofessional conduct. The physician sued the department chairperson for defamation. The suit was dismissed, the court holding that the physician's request for specification of charges was a consent that created an absolute privilege on behalf of the chairperson to communicate without liability. [*Schechet v. Kesten*, 141 N.W.2d 641 (Mich. Ct. App. 1966)]

Written consent to communication contained in the application for medical staff membership will serve to emphasize to the practitioner and to the members of the medical staff engaged in performing review and evaluation that an open communication concerning deficiencies is intended and that each member of the medical staff voluntarily submits to the review procedure.

Once otherwise defamatory remarks have been made, the affected practitioner may explicitly or implicitly consent to their further publication and, by so doing, waive his or her right to recover.

Privilege: Whether the practitioner consented to the publication of defamatory remarks may be of limited consequence in hospital peer review activities because of the existence of privilege concerning statements made within the scope of review.

Most of the cases involving defamation against a hospital or its medical staff members acting in an administrative capacity have been resolved in favor of the hospital or medical staff officer on the basis that the alleged defamatory remarks were privileged.

Privilege in hospital review matters has been characterized as both absolute and qualified. An absolute privilege is an exemption from liability for defamatory statements on the basis that public policy requires complete immunity in order to satisfy society's need for unfettered communication—even though false and malicious statements might be made—in some areas of vital public concern. Hospital medical staff review and disciplinary proceedings have been defined as vital to the public welfare so that such proceedings may enjoy an absolute privilege in some states. In other states, the privilege is considered qualified. A qualified privilege is an exemption from liability for defamatory statements made in good faith in communications concerning subjects in which the party communicating has an interest or a duty to communicate to another with a corresponding interest or responsibility. Statements made by hospital administrators, members of the governing body, and members of the medical staff about an applicant for medical staff membership or a member of the hospital's medical staff have been held to be qualifiedly privileged when made in good faith to others with a legitimate interest in the physician's performance or qualifications.

Q.1:38 What is malicious interference with contract, trade, business, or profession?

A practitioner may attempt to sue a hospital for the economic harm caused by the denial or restriction of staff privileges by alleging malicious interference with contract, trade, business, or profession. To prove interference with a contractual relation, the practitioner must prove that there was a valid contract between the practitioner and another party, that the peer reviewers had knowledge of the contract and intentionally and maliciously induced the breach of that contract, that the contract was breached due to the peer reviewers' actions, and that the practitioner was damaged.

This type of action is generally not successful. In one case, for example, a court ruled that unless the practitioner can prove the agent or officer of the hospital acted out of personal motives, that person cannot be held liable for interference with the practitioner's relationship with the hospital. [*Murray v. Bridgeport Hospital*, 480 A.2d 610 (Conn. Super. 1984)]

In another case, a court rejected a claim that members of peer review committees, administration, and boards interfered with the physician's "contract" with a hospital. The court found that the hospital itself made the decision to deny privileges. [*Buckner v. Lower Florida Keys Hospital District*, 403 So.2d 1025 (Fla. App. 1981)]

In one case, however, a pathologist was awarded $19 million in punitive damages against a hospital that economically injured him by wrongfully interfering with the contractual relationship he had with referring physicians. The court upheld the jury award. It found that the physician had established by substantial evidence that the hospital had interfered with his contractual relationships and that he had suffered damages. It recognized the enormity of the award but ruled that the jury was fully capable of determining the true motivation behind the hospital's activities. The jury determined that there was "a degree of recklessness, and malice and outright revenge that came into play. . . ." The court therefore refused to overturn the jury's determination. [*American Medical International, Inc. v. Scheller*, 590 So.2d 947 (Fla. Dist. Ct. App. 1991)]

Q.1:39 What are the antitrust laws designed to do?

Broadly speaking, the antitrust laws are intended to remedy abuses associated with the acquisition of market power. If one entity acquires and maintains too much market power and there is little or no competition, consumers may consequently suffer economic harm. Market power can be acquired and maintained legitimately by any competitor in the market. Antitrust concerns are raised, however, when a single entity employs unfair methods to acquire or maintain market power or when two or more entities combine to aggregate their market power. Any practice that could arguably affect competition may be subject to antitrust scrutiny.

Q.1:40 What are the antitrust concerns?

Physicians may view any adverse action taken with respect to a hospital staff member or an applicant for staff membership as anticompetitive. Cases have been brought under the antitrust laws to challenge exclusions, expulsions, and suspensions from staff as well as other limitations placed on a practitioner's use of hospital facilities. In addition, alleged exclusions from referral lists have been challenged as has exclusion from an emergency department on-call roster. Any action that impinges on a practitioner's unfettered right to practice may be the subject of an antitrust challenge.

The type of restraint imposed is significant under the antitrust laws. Even if the purpose of a restraint is legitimate, courts may inquire into whether there is a less restrictive alternative that could accomplish the same result.

Interstate Commerce

To establish an antitrust violation, the Sherman Act requires that the illegal restraint of trade affect interstate commerce. The federal circuit courts have been in disagreement over the type of nexus between defendants' activities and interstate commerce that will establish a substantial effect on interstate commerce. Several courts have required that the particular business activity being challenged have an effect on interstate commerce. Other courts have held, however, that any of the hospital's general interstate business activities will satisfy the interstate commerce requirement.

Rule of Reason

Restrictive hospital staffing decisions should, for the most part, be considered under the rule of reason. The difficulty with cases involving staff privileges is that hospitals and their staffs may have independent interests in restricting staff privileges. For example, a hospital may want to restrict the practice of nurse anesthetists for quality-of-care reasons, while the medical staff may want to restrict the practice of nurse anesthetists for anticompetitive reasons.

It is not always clear whether the interest of the hospital or the interest of the staff predominates in staff restrictions. The rule of reason is particularly well suited to situations such as the credentialing process, in which many different interests are at stake. Moreover, it has often been applied to the credential requirements and restrictions imposed on members of professional associations. Courts may, under the rule of reason, "weigh all of the circumstances of [the] case in deciding whether a restrictive practice should be prohibited as imposing an unreasonable restraint on competition." [*Continental Television, Inc. v. GTE Sylvania, Inc.*, 433 U.S. 36 (1977) at 49]

Market

A physician alleging an antitrust violation must establish the relevant product and geographic markets. The product market is typically defined by the specialty in which the physician practices, but may be broader if other types of physicians provide similar services. The geographic market will vary depending on the scope of the physician's practice. For example, one case held that a pathologist practiced in a national market.

Anticompetitive Effect

In determining anticompetitive effect, the focus is on the entire marketplace, not on the physician's practice. If there are other facilities at which the physician can practice and there are other physicians to whom patients can go, there will be no finding of anticompetitive effect.

2

Participants in the Credentialing Process

Q.2:1 Who does the credentialing in a hospital?

The governing body, hospital administration, the medical staff through the medical executive committee, the credentials committee, and the clinical department chair all play a role in the credentialing process. In addition, other health care providers and other committees contribute valuable information regarding provider performance that is essential in properly evaluating providers.

Members of the administrative staff gather the information necessary for making membership and privileging decisions. Before consideration of individual applications, physicians in the appropriate clinical departments or services provide information to the credentials committee on the level of training and experience required to perform specific procedures so that the credentials committee can establish appropriate membership and credentialing criteria. The chair of the appropriate clinical department reviews each application and makes a recommendation for privilege delineation. Other hospital providers or committees, such as the quality assessment and utilization management committees, submit information to the credentials committee to be used for monitoring the quality of care and for reappointment and privileging decisions. The credentials committee establishes criteria for membership and privileging, reviews the pertinent information regarding individuals, and makes its recommendations to the medical executive committee. The medical executive committee reviews the information and makes its recommendations to the governing body, which makes the final credentialing decisions.

Q.2:2 What is the governing body and what is its role in credentialing?

The governing body, often termed the board of directors or the board of trustees, is the ultimate authority in the hospital, whether the hospital is structured as a for-profit or a not-for-profit corporation. A hospital governing body's creation and organization is subject not only to traditional constraints, such as the corporate charter and corporation statutes, but also to extraordinary conditions imposed by licensure as a hospital and participation as a provider hospital under federal health programs. The hospital's articles of incorporation, or hospital bylaws, set out the organizational structure of the hospital and provide the blueprint for how the organization will be run.

It is the governing body that makes strategic decisions that will determine how the hospital will do business. For example, it is the governing body that adopts a medical staff development plan and decides whether the hospital will have an open or closed medical staff and whether the hospital will enter into exclusive contracts.

Final credentialing decisions regarding membership and privileges are made at the governing body level. The members of the governing body, however, while they have ultimate responsibility for making such decisions, do not have the clinical knowledge necessary for evaluating or re-evaluating the clinical performance of medical staff members. The Joint Commission states that the medical staff executive committee is responsible for making recommendations to the governing body regarding the mechanism by which membership and privileging decisions will be made, [GB 1.11 (1994)] and for making recommendations regarding membership and privileging as applied to particular individuals. [MS 4.1.2 (1994)] The governing body does not, however, serve a rubber stamp function for the medical staff but must function independently and make its own decisions after considering input from the medical staff.

Q.2:3 How are governing boards regulated?

State corporation laws, which vary somewhat from jurisdiction to jurisdiction, apply to hospitals and specify the parameters of their powers and responsibilities. In addition, regulations promulgated pursuant to state hospital licensure statutes may contain provisions referencing governing boards. For example, Indiana licensing regulations state that the hospital governing board is the supreme authority in the hospital. [Ind. Code §16-21-2-25 (1993)] North Carolina licensing regulations require that hospital governing boards appoint the physician staff on a nondiscriminatory basis. [N.C. Gen. Stat. §131E-85(a) (1992)] Michigan regulations set out the license requirements and the duties of the governing board. [Mich. Comp. Law §§333.21511–333.21513 (1992)]

Federal regulations as well are directed toward defining the organization and procedures of hospital governing boards. The Conditions of Participation for hospitals promulgated under the Medicare program, which are applicable to all providers that have Medicare participation agreements, require a hospital to have an effective governing body legally responsible for the conduct of the institution. [42 C.F.R. §482.1] The governing body must appoint members of the medical staff and a chief executive officer (CEO), ensure that patients are under the care of appropriate practitioners, and formulate an institutional plan and budget. In addition, the governing body is responsible for services furnished in the hospital whether or not they are furnished under contract.

The Joint Commission also has standards regarding the governing body. The standards spell out the responsibilities of the governing body, state how it should be organized, and indicate what the governing body's bylaws, rules, and regulations should contain.

Q.2:4 What is a typical profile of a governing board?

Just as hospitals vary considerably in size, purpose, and make-up, so do their boards. The average hospital board today has 17 members, the smaller boards may have eight or nine members, and the larger boards have around 25 members. Typically, the board's composition is dominated by business executives but may include members of the legal and accounting professions. Physicians often serve with no voting power but as representatives of the medical staff. Interest and commitment to the hospital followed by financial business skills are the leading criteria for selecting trustees. Trustees are frequently chosen from among the more prominent members of the community. It is not uncommon to find representatives of well-established families with inherited wealth serving on boards. A more recent trend, however, has been one of providing community or consumer representation on boards. Yet, for the most part, the traditional character of the board still holds. With regard to the age of a typical board member, over 55 percent fall between the ages of 51 and 70, and 38 percent between the ages of 31 and 50. The majority of board members have a business or health care background. Some 87 percent of the hospitals have CEOs as board members, but only 36 percent have granted the CEO voting privileges. Board membership is predominantly male, although across the United States, only 8.3 percent of boards are exclusively male.

Hospital boards typically meet between 10 and 12 times a year, usually on a monthly basis. This is reasonable considering a board may not meet during one of the summer months or during the holiday season. Board terms vary considerably, but the average term of membership is slightly in excess of three years, with a majority of hospitals stipulating no limit on the number of consecutive terms a board member may serve. (Snook, I.D., *Hospitals: What They Are and How They Work*. Gaithersburg, MD: Aspen Publishers, Inc., 1992, 26; 27)

Q.2:5 If the hospital is part of a health care system and there is a hospital board and a parent company board, who has final say in credentialing matters?

The organizing documents of the health care system will indicate the division of authority. The local governing body generally retains primary responsibility for key medical staff issues. There are many issues with multiple hospital systems, especially those that cross state lines. Peer review and credentialing laws vary state by state, and the ability to retain authority by an out of state parent company may be limited by varying state licensure, confidentiality/peer review laws, and credentialing laws.

Q.2:6 What is the medical executive committee and what is its role in the credentialing process?

The medical executive committee comprises a group of medical staff members that represent and act on behalf of the entire medical staff in most matters (except election of officers and adoption or amendment of the bylaws, which require full staff participation). The medical executive committee comprises voting and nonvoting members. The voting members are elected by the medical staff and are often medical staff leaders, such as clinical department chairpersons. The nonvoting members may include the CEO and a representative from nursing administration or other individuals as specified in the medical staff bylaws.

The duties of the medical executive committee are spelled out in detail in the medical staff bylaws. In the credentialing context, the medical executive committee receives recommendations from the credentialing committee and recommends to the governing body all matters relating to appointments, reappointments, staff category and department assignments, and clinical privileges. It also plays a vital role in corrective actions. (See **Chapter 6**.)

Q.2:7 What is the credentials committee?

The credentials committee is composed of members of the medical staff who establish the standards for membership and credentialing, then evaluate completed applications for initial appointment, clinical privileges, reappointment, and renewal or addition of clinical privileges. The credentials committee makes its recommendations to the medical executive committee.

Q.2:8 What is a medical staff services department or a medical staff office?

Larger facilities will have a medical staff services department (MSSD) to assist the medical staff in carrying out its functions by rendering administrative support, while smaller facilities generally will have at least a medical staff office (MSO) to assume these responsibilities. Organizationally, both the MSSD and the MSO are arms of the hospital administration.

The MSSD and the MSO can be organized in many different ways, depending on the needs of the institution. The number of employees as well as the range of responsibilities vary from institution to institution. These responsibilities may include continuing medical education, graduate medical education, physician referral, recruitment, marketing, and credentialing, and may even extend to risk management and quality assurance in some facilities.

While the MSSD or the MSO works very closely with the medical staff, they are creations of the hospital and report to hospital administration. Personnel in these departments are employees of the hospital and are evaluated by administrative personnel. In some instances, the MSSD or the MSO is supported in part by the collection of medical staff dues and may report to the institution's chief of staff, whose salary may also be partially provided by the medical staff. In this case, the MSSD or the MSO is viewed as more closely aligned with the medical staff.

Q.2:9 What other entities credential practitioners?

- MCOs, such as HMOs, must make decisions regarding who will be allowed to participate in the particular MCO.
- Physician Hospital Organizations (PHOs) often assume credentialing responsibilities. PHOs are organizations that form alliances between hospitals and physicians mainly for the purpose of pursuing managed care contracts. They may also provide billing and management information system services and develop utilization review and quality assurance programs.
- MSOs are organizations that typically provide various services to physicians, although there are freestanding, hospital-affiliated, physician-affiliated, joint venture (hospital/physician), and MCO models. MSOs may provide all of the services of a PHO, including credentialing and more.

- Large group practices and IPAs also perform credentialing. When an IPA contracts with a managed care plan, the responsibility for credentialing may be delegated to the IPA.
- Medical societies often perform credentialing, which hospitals and other health care organizations can access.

3

Criteria for Medical Staff Membership

Q.3:1 Must criteria for medical staff membership be defined in writing?

The Joint Commission indicates that criteria for granting initial or continuing staff membership must be "specified in the medical staff bylaws and uniformly applied to all applicants for medical staff membership." [MS 2.4.1]

Q.3:2 What are some basic ground rules for establishing criteria?

Credentialing criteria should be objective and have a rational relationship to the hospital's business and quality of care concerns. Objective criteria will be better accepted by both the reviewers and the reviewed and, as long as they are consistently applied, will provide a solid basis for defense of decisions to exclude various providers.

Q.3:3 What are the externally established criteria for admission to the medical staff?

Most criteria for medical staff membership are established internally, by the facility. A few criteria are established by external factors, such as state law. Examples of externally established criteria are those pertaining to education and licensure, which are fundamental criteria for admission to the medical staff. Some states and the HCQIA require that, as part of the appointment process, hospitals query the state medical licensing board and/or the NPDB to discover whether there has been any disciplinary action taken against the applicant. [See Alaska Stat. §18.20.076.] Basic to the practice of medicine is the satisfaction of underlying educational requirements. The requirement of an appropriate education is fundamental to medical staff appointment. The type and duration of schooling demanded for each profession is dictated by agreement among the educational establishment, the profession speaking through its organized associations, and the government as represented by the licensing agency. Basic educational requirements are normally noted in licensing legislation, and hospitals may use these laws for guidance.

State law requires that practitioners possess a valid state license in order to provide health care services. A hospital that knowingly permits an unlicensed physician to practice on its premises may be liable for aiding and abetting the illegal practice of medicine and potentially for any malpractice committed by the individual if the harm inflicted may have been avoided through licensure. Exceptions may be made for members of medical school faculties, the granting of emergency privileges, and physicians working in federal or state institutions.

To ensure that the hospital is fully informed as to licensure, practitioners should be required to agree to report any revocation or suspension or other restriction of their licenses as part of the conditions for admission to and continued membership on medical staff. It is advisable for the medical staff to require its members to provide confirmation of licensure on a periodic basis.

Q.3:4 Can a hospital adopt criteria more stringent than those required by state or federal law or the Joint Commission?

Yes, a hospital can adopt more stringent criteria as long as the criteria are reasonably related to the hospital's business purpose.

Q.3:5 Can ability to work with others be used as a criterion for admission to the medical staff?

Absolutely. Delivery of health care is accomplished by a team of professionals working together. A health care professional who is disruptive can damage the effectiveness of this health care delivery team. There is a substantial body of case law that supports using the ability to work with others as a criterion for admission to the staff as well as a ground for disciplinary action.

For example, West Virginia's highest court ruled in a 1991 case that disruptive conduct is a legitimate reason for revocation of privileges, that the bylaws were not too vague on that point, and that a hospital need not wait for a physician to harm a patient before revoking his or her privileges. [*Mahmoodian v. United Hospital Center Inc.*, 404 S.E.2d 750 (W. Va. 1991) *cert. denied*, 60 U.S.L.W. 3262 (Oct. 7, 1991)] The court reasoned that a hospital has not only a right but a duty to ensure that physicians appointed to the medical staff meet certain standards of professional competence and professional conduct as long as the standards are linked to quality of care.

The case arose after a private hospital revoked a physician's medical staff privileges because of his repeatedly disruptive behavior. Among the allegations were that the physician refused to give verbal orders to the registered nurses with whom he was feuding, interfered with a lymph node biopsy being performed by his "arch rival" by striding into the operating room and demanding that the operation be stopped, and refused to come to the hospital at the request of a resident to evaluate a patient who had been in labor for 16 hours.

In that case, the medical staff bylaws stated that corrective action could be taken if the conduct of a practitioner is "disruptive to the operations of the hospital." Another bylaw provision indicated that one of the qualifications for membership on staff was "an ability to work with others" to ensure that patients treated by a physician will be given a high quality of medical care. The court found these bylaw provisions to set forth a reasonably definite standard of professional conduct that gives physicians sufficient notice as to what is expected of them. Finally, the court held that while disruptive conduct must be tied to patient care, a hospital need not wait until actual harm is done before acting.

Other decisions have upheld:

- a hospital's rejection of an application due to the applicant's failure to document his ability to work with others [*Huffaker v. Bailey*, 540 P.2d 1398 (Or. 1975)]
- the removal of oral surgeons from an emergency call roster because of their inability to work in harmony with the hospital's department chairman [*Grodjesk v. Jersey City Medical Center*, 343 A.2d 489 (N.J. Super. 1975)]
- the denial of reappointment to a medical staff member because of generally disruptive behavior toward other members of the medical staff, nurses, and the hospital administration [*Silver v. Queen's Hosp.*, 629 P.2d 1116 (Haw. 1981)]
- the summary suspension of a psychiatrist's hospital privileges after he consistently failed to attend mandatory departmental patient staffing conferences. [*Cipriotti v. Board of Directors of Northridge Hosp. Found. Medical Center*, 196 Cal. Rptr. 367 (Ct. App. 1983)]

Q.3:6 Can school of practice be used as a criterion for staff membership or privileges?

It depends on what type of practitioner is involved and on what state law specifies. The practitioners most commonly affected by school of practice restrictions have been osteopathic physicians, podiatrists, and chiropractors.

- In California, the rules of each health facility must provide for use of the facility and staff privileges for "duly licensed podiatrists within the scope of their . . . licensure." [Cal. Health & Safety Code §1316]

- New Mexico provides by statute for equality of treatment regarding medical staff privileges for osteopathic and medical physicians. [N.M. Stat. Ann. §61-10-14]
- Missouri has a broadly drawn statute that states that discrimination between practitioners of the various schools of medicine is prohibited and grants patients the right to be treated by the physician of their choice. [Mo. Rev. Stat. §205.300]
- Laws in the District of Columbia, New York, and Florida specify that health care facilities may not exclude from consideration for medical staff membership certified nurse practitioners, podiatrists, and psychologists. [D.C. Code Ann §32-1307; N.Y. Pub. Health Law §2801-b; Fla. Stat. Ann. §395.011]

Case law generally indicates that osteopathic physicians may not be automatically excluded from medical staff membership, and any exclusion may be tested for its reasonableness in light of the background and capabilities of the osteopath-applicant. [See, e.g., *Berman v. Florida Medical Center*, 600 F.2d 466 (5th Cir. 1979).] Many state statutes, such as the New Mexico law mentioned above, also forbid discrimination against osteopaths.

Podiatrists and chiropractors seeking medical staff appointment have been confronted by a greater obstacle than have osteopathic physicians simply because their schools of practice are much more restricted in scope in comparison.

In one case, a podiatrist alleged denial of equal protection because podiatrists as a class were prohibited from holding medical staff membership in a hospital. [*Shaw v. Hospital Authority of Cobb County*, 507 F.2d 625 (5th Cir. 1975)] The podiatrist argued that all practitioners of the healing arts should be accorded equal treatment. The court rejected this premise, finding that all classes of practitioners of the healing arts do not have equal competence to perform as members of a hospital medical staff. (The court did find, however, that the podiatrist was entitled to procedural due process relative to his application.) In a New Hampshire case, a federal court ruled that a hospital's refusal to grant privileges to podiatrists does not violate federal or state constitutions. [*New*

Hampshire Podiatric Medical Assoc. v. New Hampshire Hosp. Assoc., 735 F. Supp. 448 (D.N.H. 1990)]

On the other hand, the Ohio Supreme Court struck down medical staff bylaws that severely restricted podiatrists' privileges and relegated them to the courtesy staff. That state's high court ruled that such treatment violated a state antidiscrimination statute. [*Dooley v. Barberton Citizen's Hospital,* 465 N.E.2d 58 (Ohio 1984)]

As is the case with osteopaths, the rights of podiatrists to medical staff membership may be protected by state statute.

Chiropractors have not won medical staff appointment through litigation, and have even failed in attempts to compel hospitals to accept referral patients for radiological and laboratory services. [See, e.g., *Fort Hamilton-Hughes Memorial Hosp. v. Southard,* 466 N.E.2d 903 (Ohio 1984).] At least one jurisdiction, however, has upheld a rule requiring radiologists to provide services to licensed chiropractors who refer patients to them. [*Brodie v. New Jersey Bd. of Medical Examiners,* 427 A.2d 104 (N.J. Super. Ct. App. Div. 1981), *aff'd,* 707 F.2d 1389 (3d Cir. 1983)]

In a 1994 case, a New Jersey court upheld a hospital's refusal to admit chiropractors to the medical staff. [*Petrocco v. Dover Gen. Hosp. & Med. Ctr.,* No. A–4378–92T5 (N.J. Super. Ct. May 20, 1994)] The court found that the hospital did more than the law required. Instead of rejecting the chiropractor's application offhandedly, it formed a committee to solicit information on the issue of whether to amend its bylaws and permit chiropractors to become staff members. The committee concluded that chiropractors were not necessary to the hospital's acute-care mission, that an insignificant number of patients would require chiropractic services, and that the administrative cost of adding chiropractors would outweigh any benefits. The court concluded that it would not second-guess the hospital's honest administrative judgment.

Q.3:7 Can applicants be required to abide by hospital rules and policies as a criterion for staff membership or privileges?

Applicants should agree to be bound by the hospital and medical staff bylaws, rules, regulations, and policies. This requirement provides a basis for discipline of a practitioner who violates hospital policies that are not directly tied to patient care but are nonetheless important, such as a hospital's sexual harassment policy. Adherence to hospital rules and policies is normally construed by the courts to be essential to the proper functioning of the hospital and a valid requirement to be imposed on members of the medical staff in light of the hospital's duty to provide quality care to its patients. The courts will uphold a hospital's refusal to appoint or reappoint a physician who fails to agree to abide by the bylaws and policies. [See, e.g., *Yeargin v. Hamilton Memorial Hosp.* 171 S.E.2d 136 (Ga. 1978).]

In addition, the Joint Commission requires that "each applicant for medical staff membership is oriented to these bylaws, rules and regulations, and policies and agrees in writing that his/her activities as a member of the medical staff will be bound by them." [MS 2.1.1 (1994)]

Q.3:8 Can applicants be required to participate in an on-call schedule for the care of emergency department patients as a criterion for staff membership or privileges?

This can be a condition of medical staff membership. On-call availability for emergency department service is commonly accepted by the medical profession as a reasonable condition of medical staff membership and has not been a matter of serious contention resulting in litigation.

Q.3:9 Can geographic proximity of office or residence be made a criterion of medical staff membership or privileges?

A reasonably drawn bylaw regarding office or residence location will probably withstand challenge as long as it is reasonably related to the hospital's duty to provide quality patient care. Possible unreasonable requirements might be: the location of office and residence in a specific geographic area; an overly restrictive geographic area, such as location within city limits; and changing geographic location rules after medical staff appointment, thereby imposing a relocation burden on the practitioner.

Interestingly, as hospitals form networks and alliances that may include geographically diverse entities to remain competitive in the changing health care environment, geographical limitations may become impractical.

Q.3:10 Can board certification or eligibility be used as a criterion for staff membership or privileges?

Board certification may be used as a criterion for staff membership or privileges. [See, e.g., *Smith v. Vallejo General Hospital*, 1770 Cal. App. 3d 450 (1985).] Whether the hospital chooses to do so is a policy decision. If this criterion is adopted, it should be because of quality of care concerns. The governing body should ensure that it is not being used as a vehicle for discrimination or unreasonable staff restriction.

The Joint Commission indicates that "[b]oard certification is an excellent benchmark and is considered when delineating clinical privileges." [MS 2.15.2 (1994)] Board certification may not be the sole criterion, however, according to the Medicare Conditions of Participation. [42 C.F.R. §482.12(a)(7) (1990)] In a Tennessee case, a court found that a public hospital's denial of surgical privileges *solely* because of the practitioner's lack of board certification or eligibility was arbitrary, capricious, discriminatory, and beyond the jurisdiction of the hospital. [*Armstrong v. Board of Directors of Fayette County Gen. Hosp.*, 553 S.W.2d 77 (Tenn. App. 1976)]

Q.3:11 Can evidence of adequate malpractice insurance be made a criterion for staff membership or privileges?

This is a well-established legitimate criterion. Some states, such as California, have enacted legislation specifically permitting hospitals to add insurance requirements to their medical staff bylaws. In addition, the courts have found this to be an appropriate criterion. In a 1986 case, for example, the Washington Supreme Court ruled that because a hospital has a compelling interest in protecting the financial interest of both patients and the hospital, the board of commissioners of a county hospital district could terminate the staff privileges of a physician who refused, for religious reasons, to comply with a hospital bylaw requiring that medical staff members obtain professional liability insurance. [*Backlund v. Board of Comm. of King County Hosp.* Dist. 2, 724 P.2d 981 (Wash. 1986)]

In a 1990 case, a court held that a hospital was justified in suspending a physician's medical staff privileges for three weeks because he had practiced for six months without malpractice insurance, in violation of the medical staff bylaws. [*Courtney v. Shore Memorial Hosp.* 584 A.2d 817 (N.J. Super. Ct. 1990)] The fact that he later obtained retroactive coverage was irrelevant according to the court.

Specifying only a certain monetary amount of insurance coverage may be inadequate to protect the hospital, other medical staff members, and hospital patients. A practitioner could obtain insurance from an insurer of questionable stability. In addition to amount of coverage, the criterion may address the source of such insurance, requiring approval of the carrier by the governing body.

Q.3:12 Can medical school faculty appointment be made a criterion for staff membership or privileges?

In the teaching hospital setting, there may be a relationship of dependency between a physician's medical staff appointment and his or her appointment to the faculty. In one case, the court ruled in favor of a hospital affiliated with the Washington University School of Medicine when reappointment of a staff physician was denied following his loss of faculty appointment. [*Dillard v. Rowland*, 520 S.W.2d 81 (Mo. App. 1974)] In its contract with the university, the hospital agreed that the medical staff of the hospital would "consist solely of the teaching corps of the university's school of medicine." When the physician refused an offer of a full-time salaried position with the medical school, preferring to remain in a part-time status that would provide him a higher income from private practice, he lost his teaching position, and consequently, his medical staff privileges at the hospital were not renewed.

The court first considered the validity of the agreement between the hospital and university requiring that the hospital's medical staff be composed solely of university faculty. The court held that the contract provision was reasonable and necessary for the successful operation of the hospital as an affiliated institution. The court also noted that the board of trustees of the hospital had the right to grant or refuse staff appointments to any physician as long as that physician held a faculty appointment in the Department of Medicine of the university.

Teaching hospitals probably have the discretion to make faculty appointment a necessary condition to the granting of medical staff privileges, but such a requirement may be subject to close scrutiny regarding its reasonableness in relation to the hospital's commitment to satisfy community needs and provide quality care.

Q.3:13 Can the provision of charity care or care of Medicaid patients be made a criterion for staff membership or privileges?

Yes, hospitals may establish requirements that staff members provide a certain amount of charity care in the institution or that they see an established number of Medicaid patients. In Pennsylvania, for example, a private, nonprofit hospital suspended the staff privileges of a physician who refused to comply with a bylaw requiring him to treat a percentage of the hospital's indigent patients. [Clair v. Centre Community Hosp. 463 A.2d 1065 (Pa. Super. Ct. 1983)] The bylaw required that the physician, who was one of three obstetrician–gynecologists on the hospital's staff, treat every third indigent ob/gyn patient at the hospital. The physician explained that he was unable to take on an unlimited number of patients and still properly care for them. He sued to prevent the hospital from suspending his staff privileges. The Pennsylvania appeals court determined that the suspension did not unconstitutionally deprive the physician of his right to practice medicine as he alleged. The bylaw, it reasoned, bears a rational relationship to the legitimate stated purpose of providing health care to the poor.

For hospitals that accepted building funds under the federal Hill Burton Act, there is a "community service" obligation that requires acceptance of indigent patients. The law also has an "uncompensated care" obligation that lasts for 20 years from the date of the Hill Burton grant. Without physicians that accept the responsibility to treat indigent patients, the hospital would be unable to fulfill its Hill Burton obligations.

Q.3:14 Can physical and mental condition be made a criterion for staff membership or privileges?

Applicants for medical staff membership should be physically and mentally fit to practice their professions in the institution. The medical staff bylaws should provide for initial evaluation of the health of an applicant for medical staff privileges as well as periodic reappraisal of mental and physical fitness. The Joint Commission has recognized the importance of the health of medical staff members, and its Medical Staff Standards include health status as a qualification for initial appointment and continued membership.

Laws that may be relevant to this issue include the ADA, the Rehabilitation Act of 1974, and state civil rights laws. [MS 2.4.1.3 (1994)] (See **Q.1:18** and **5:15** for further discussion of this criterion.)

Q.3:15 Can utilization patterns be made a criterion for staff membership or privileges?

Reasonable economic considerations are acceptable. As hospitals become increasingly aware of cost containment, a physician's ability to work within economic constraints while continuing to provide quality medical care is becoming an important criterion in medical staff privilege decisions. For example, a New Jersey trial court ruled that a hospital's denial of staff privileges to a physician who had a history of excessive utilization of hospital beds and who repeatedly failed to meet professional standards review organization criteria for length of stay and appropriate admissions was not arbitrary, capricious, or unreasonable. [*Edelman v. John F. Kennedy*

Hosp. No. C-2104-80 (N.J. Super Ct. June 25, 1982), *cert. denied,* 475 A.2d 585 (N.J. 1984)]

As PHOs proliferate and as they desire long-term and risk-sharing arrangements with MCOs, this area will become increasingly important.

Q.3:16 Have any criteria been considered invalid?

Any criteria based on discriminatory grounds, such as race, national origin, sex, or religion, are obviously illegal and would be struck down.

The New Jersey Supreme Court found invalid a hospital policy that denied medical staff privileges to physicians who had not practiced medicine in the hospital's service area for more than two years. [*Berman v. Valley Hosp.,* 510 A.2d 673 (N.J. 1986)]

State licensure statutes may indicate that certain criteria are not valid. The District of Columbia law, for example, lists the following as invalid criteria:

- applicant's membership in a professional association
- decision to advertise
- participation in a prepaid group health plan
- certain practices with regard to testifying in malpractice suits [D.C. Code 1981 §32-1307 (1993)]

4

Delineation of Clinical Privileges

Q.4:1 What are clinical privileges?

The Joint Commission defines clinical privileges as "permission to provide medical or other patient care services in the granting institution, within well-defined limits, based on the individual's professional license and his/her experience, competence, ability, and judgment." [MS 1 (1994)] The delineation of an individual's clinical privileges includes the limitations, if any, on an individual's privileges to admit and treat patients or direct the course of treatment for the conditions for which the patients were admitted. [MS 2.16 (1994)]

Q.4:2 What is "delineation of privileges?"

Delineation of privileges is a term that is used in several ways. The term is used to describe the process of establishing specific criteria a practitioner must meet to perform specific procedures at a hospital. Each member of the medical staff is measured against these criteria, which are developed by each clinical department or specialty practicing in the hospital. As each practitioner is evaluated, the scope of practice is outlined and appropriate privileges are granted. The term delineation of privileges is also used to refer to the granting of specific privileges to each practitioner.

Q.4:3 Is the delineation or granting of clinical privileges regulated by law?

State statutes or administrative codes may list various requirements concerning the delineation of privileges. California law, for example, states that "A committee of the medical staff shall be assigned responsibility for recommending to the governing body the delineation of medical privileges." [Cal. Regs. at 22 CCR 90203(a)(1)]

In Florida, the regulations contain the following two provisions. "The governing authority shall require a delineation of privileges for each member of the organized medical staff." [FAC §59A-3.156(4)(d)] "The delineation of privileges shall not be stated simply as a specialty designator, such as "general surgery" or "general medicine" unless such terms are specifically defined elsewhere." [FAC §59A-2.156 (4)(d)]

Q.4:4 Must a practitioner requesting privileges prove that he or she is qualified to perform the procedures for which privileges are requested?

It is the practitioner's responsibility to prove that he or she has received the necessary education, training, and experience to be granted the requested privileges. The application form should require the practitioner to submit evidence of competence. This evidence will be evaluated against the criteria that have been established by the department and approved by the governing board.

Q.4:5 When are clinical privileges criteria defined?

Clinical privileges criteria should be defined before applications for those privileges are accepted. There should be a documented procedure for establishing criteria, and it should be strictly followed. Ensuring that the procedure and the implementation of the procedure are objective will deflect charges of bias and anticompetitive motives in the establishment of the criteria.

A 1991 case involved the *ex post facto* development of criteria for scrub nurses. There were no privileging criteria established for private-duty scrub nurses. There were multiple problems with a private-duty scrub nurse who had been granted temporary privileges. The hospital subsequently adopted privileging criteria that effectively eliminated the possibility that the nurse would receive privileges. She sued, claiming that the criteria was adopted in retaliation for a prior discrimination action. The court ruled that

". . . the discriminatory act was the application of these new higher standards to [the nurse] by the Executive Committee and other decision makers. It was this application of the standards which differed substantially from the bases upon which [the hospital] had in the past hired scrub nurses into its own employment which evidenced [the hospital's] discriminatory purpose." [*Christopher v. Stouder Mem. Hosp.*, 936 F.2d 870 (6th Cir.), at p. 879, *cert. denied*, 112 S. Ct. 658 (1991)]

Q.4:6 How are criteria for granting clinical privileges developed?

The criteria are developed by each department or service. The department or service chairperson must define what information is needed and must set the criteria for evaluating practitioners, not only initially, but on an ongoing basis as well. The criteria may apply not only to clinical factors but may also include elements related to how the practitioner carries out departmental and facility-wide responsibilities, such as attendance at medical staff meetings and adherence to medical staff and hospital policies. The chairperson will be asked to evaluate overall performance on the basis of these factors as well as clinical competence.

The use of established objective criteria makes the process easier to manage and less subject to challenge. Several medical specialty groups, such as the American College of Physicians (ACP), have developed guidelines for clinical competence in specific medical procedures, which are intended to be used as minimum criteria necessary for competent performance of such procedures. As stated in *Annals of Internal Medicine*, the ACP guidelines strive to be neutral in terms of medical specialty, geographic location, and type of practice. They describe minimum competence for the beginner treating an average patient. The ACP indicates that, in some instances, a minimum number of procedures in order to attain competence is indicated. However, quantity should never be the sole or main criterion for competence, which also involves cognitive skills and the total educational experience. [*Annals of Internal Medicine*, 1987; 107:585-7]

In addition to checking with professional specialty groups in establishing criteria, the department or service may check with training programs or the university teaching hospital where the procedure was first performed.

For experimental procedures and drugs, sources for protocol requirements/development include the Food and Drug Administration (FDA) and the National Cancer Institute (NCI). In some cases, such as drugs not yet approved by the FDA, compliance may be required. There are also specific protocols for patient disclosure and consent.

Many universities have their own clinical trials that are not NCI-sponsored or approved. When state law does not mandate coverage for these types of trials, insurers and MCOs may only pay for NCI-approved trials, resulting in an economic impact on the hospital and the patient.

In a university setting, there are many new procedures being developed. Therefore, it may be harder to have established criteria, but it is vital because of the chance of an incident of medical malpractice arising with a new procedure.

Q.4:7 How are criteria established if the procedure can be performed by specialists in different departments or services?

There are some procedures that can be performed by members of different departments. These departments should work together in establishing criteria for such procedures. Through consensus-building between departments or services, there should be development of one set of criteria for crossover privileging. If there is disagreement that the medical staff leadership cannot resolve, the final determination should lie with the governing body.

Q.4:8 What if the procedure is new?

In the case of a new procedure, the hospital can inform the physician requesting privileges to perform the procedure that it is not currently being performed at the facility, but that the hospital will consider whether it will be performed there in the future. The physician should be informed that if the hospital determines that the procedure will be performed at the hospital, criteria will be established within a specified time. After criteria are established, the hospital will then reconsider the request.

In deciding whether to permit a new procedure to be performed in the hospital, there are several factors that should be considered, including:

- if the hospital has adequate facilities and support services
- if the procedure fits in with the mission statement and long-term goals of the facility
- if there is a need in the community and if other facilities are performing the procedure
- if the medical staff can properly delineate criteria and subsequently monitor the performance of practitioners performing the procedure
- in the case of experimental procedures, if the protocols for the procedure are approved by the FDA, the NCI, or other appropriate body and if both the facility and the practitioners can fulfill the protocols.

The hospital may place the burden on the practitioner who is seeking privileges to perform a new procedure to aid the MSO and the committee in gathering information to assess whether to approve the procedure and how to establish criteria for delineation of privileges.

Q.4:9 Who approves the criteria and grants clinical privileges?

The clinical department or service sends its criteria recommendations to the medical executive committee, which makes recommendations to the governing body. The medical executive committee must ensure that the recommendations stem from effective methods of monitoring clinical performance, gathering information from outside sources, and considering requests for privileges in light of facility and departmental capabilities.

The governing body approves the criteria that are recommended through the medical staff. According to *Annals of Internal Medicine*, the governing body should ensure, among other things, that

- the privilege delineation process bases recommendations on objective information on a practitioner's clinical competence, contribution to the hospital, and ability to work with others,
- departments making judgments about the same type of care use comparable professional criteria,
- recommendations for clinical privileges are not made from economic or anticompetitive motives,
- information about current facility capabilities and future plans are incorporated into the privilege delineation process,
- there is adequate financial protection for those who organize or participate in good faith quality assurance and privilege delineation.

["Privilege Delineation in a Demanding New Environment." *Annals of Internal Medicine*. Roberts, Radany, and Nash. 1988; 108]

Q.4:10 What type of procedures might require specific criteria development?

High-volume procedures, problem-prone procedures, or high tech procedures may require the development of specific criteria that must be met before the practitioner can perform the procedure.

Q.4:11 Should criteria be periodically reviewed?

The criteria should be periodically reviewed because medicine is an evolving process, and new technologies and treatment modes may require changes to the criteria. The criteria are pivotal in disciplinary actions and in litigation and, therefore, should be reviewed and updated as needed.

Q.4:12 How does a practitioner apply for clinical privileges?

A practitioner must complete a privilege delineation form. The form may be designed in several different ways. It may list the procedures, use a categorical approach, be based on board certification, or use a combination of approaches. [For a detailed discussion, see **Q.5:9.**]

Q.4:13 Who may be granted admitting privileges?

Only medical staff members are granted the privilege to admit patients to inpatient services. [MS 2.26.1 (1994)] Nonphysician members of the medical staff may be granted privileges to admit patients to inpatient services, but such patients must be given prompt medical evaluation by a qualified physician. [MS 2.16.2.1 (1994)]

Q.4:14 When are practitioners granted temporary privileges?

Temporary privileges may be granted to an applicant for membership on the medical staff whose appointment to one of those categories has not yet been considered by the governing body. All other steps in the credentialing process, except governing body approval, should have been satisfactorily completed before temporary privileges are granted. Temporary privileges in this case are granted for such period as is necessary for the governing body to act on the recommendation of the medical staff. While holding temporary privileges, the practitioner is assigned to a department where medical competence, ethics, and conduct may be observed by members of the active medical staff, usually the appropriate department chairperson or designated monitors, until such time as the governing body appoints him or her to the associate staff.

Temporary medical staff privileges also may be granted for a limited period to practitioners who have not applied for medical staff membership. This is normally done only in time of emergency or when *locum tenens* is required. Recommendation by the appropriate department chairperson, the president of the medical staff, or others usually is required. Under such conditions, a member of the active staff is required to assume monitoring responsibility for the practitioner during the limited period in which privileges are granted. All requirements regarding the granting of temporary privileges should be spelled out in the medical staff bylaws and should be adhered to strictly.

In a 1994 case, a hospital was charged with negligence for granting temporary privileges to a physician. The physician requested temporary privileges to perform a laparoscopic cholecystectomy (removal of the gall bladder using a laparascope). [*Candler General Hospital v. Persaud*, 442 S.E.2d 775 (Ga. Ct. App. 1994)] He submitted a certificate of completion of a workshop on that procedure, which he had taken five days before. The president of the hospital granted temporary privileges the same day they were requested. The patient subsequently bled to death, and her family sued the hospital for negligence in permitting the physician to perform the procedure without having instituted any standards, training requirements, or protocols or otherwise devising a method for judging the surgeon's qualification. The family alleged that the hospital knew or should have known that it did not have a credentialing process that could have assured the hospital of the physician's education, training, and ability to perform the procedure.

The court refused to dismiss the case, holding that the question of whether the hospital was negligent in granting the requested privileges must be addressed. The court pointed out that the issue was not whether the hospital was negligent in either its appointment or retention of the physician on the surgical staff. The hospital owed a duty to the patient, however, to act in good faith and with reasonable care to ensure that the surgeon was qualified to practice the procedure he was granted privileges to perform, the court concluded, and a trier of fact must determine whether the hospital failed to meet its duty in this instance.

Q.4:15 Is there a time limit for temporary privileges?

If a hospital decides that it will permit the granting of temporary privileges under certain circumstances, the bylaws should indicate a specific time period after which the temporary privileges expire. This will eliminate the necessity of a hearing to terminate the privileges.

Q.4:16 What is the advantage of having a specialist advise the board of a small or rural hospital as to whether a particular practitioner who may be lacking qualifications should be granted privileges for a specific procedure?

If the hospital grants privileges and is later charged with corporate negligence for granting privileges because a patient injury occurs, the specialist's opinion that the grant of privileges was appropriate will weigh in favor of the hospital. On the other hand, if the hospital denies privileges and the physician sues because of the denial, the specialist's unfavorable recommendation will strengthen the hospital's position. [In *Issues in Hospital Law: Selected Key Articles from Hospital Law Newsletter*, N. Hershey, "Fine-Tuning Surgical Privileges." Gaithersburg, MD: Aspen Publishers, Inc., 1989; 15]

Q.4:17 Does the hospital have to query the NPDB when an individual already on staff requests additional clinical privileges?

Yes, the NPDB must be queried when there is a request for additional privileges.

5

The Credentialing Process

Q.5:1 Where are the requirements of the credentialing process usually detailed?

The credentialing process is most often elaborated in the medical staff bylaws. Some health law attorneys recommend that the credentialing procedures be located in a separate policy document rather than in the bylaws. In fact, some attorneys recommend that there be three documents: medical staff bylaws, appointment procedures, and the fair hearing procedures. (See, e.g., James Hall, comments at NHLA Medical Staff Relations Seminar, 1993.)

Q.5:2 What is the advantage of putting the credentialing procedures in a separate policy document?

The process for amending medical staff bylaws is usually cumbersome in that amendments to the bylaws are made only with the consensus of the entire medical staff. If there is a change in the law that impacts on the credentialing procedures, such as new state legislation or case law, changing the bylaws to reflect legal requirements becomes a lengthy process. Amendments to a policy document containing credentialing procedures can be accomplished with approval of the credentials committee, executive committee, and governing board, a much expedited process.

Q.5:3 Are there disadvantages to putting the procedures in other documents?

Physicians may strongly object to making the credentialing process easier to amend as the process has a very significant effect on them. If the decision is made to move the credentialing procedures out of the bylaws and into a separate document, medical staff leaders will have to gain the trust of the medical staff and convince them that it is in their best interest to have the credentialing process in a separate document.

The Medicare Conditions of Participation appear to require credentialing procedures to be in the bylaws, but some health law attorneys interpret this as meaning that the bylaws must address the issue. The bylaws may indicate that the procedures are set forth in a separate policy. Similarly, although the Joint Commission standards contain an apparent conflict with the idea of using a separate policy, careful drafting of the bylaws can overcome this problem. Hospitals have passed the Joint Commission inspections while using separate documents.

Q.5:4 What is a fair hearing plan?

A fair hearing plan is the document that sets out the due process procedures that are triggered when a hospital denies or otherwise adversely affects a practitioner's medical staff membership or clinical privileges. The fair hearing plan should not be included within the medical staff bylaws but should be a separate policy that can be amended more easily than the bylaws.

PREAPPLICATION

Q.5:5 What is a preapplication process?

Many health care facilities have decided to employ a preapplication process in which candidates for staff membership are sent a list of membership criteria and an explanation of the credentialing process. The candidate can then assess the criteria and determine eligibility. If the candidate meets the criteria, he or she can request an application form and the application process begins.

Another alternative is that the facility can send a preapplication form to be filled out by potential applicants. If this procedure is used, the completed preapplication forms should be reviewed by administrative rather than medical personnel so that the preapplication process is clearly distinguished from the application process itself. The criteria should be objective and applied uniformly to all potential applicants. Rejection of the candidate at this phase should not trigger any hearing or appeal rights.

Q.5:6 Why have a preapplication process?

The application process is a time-consuming and costly process. The preapplication process screens out potential applicants who are not eligible, thereby saving time in processing applications. A practitioner can determine from the preapplication process whether he or she has the level of training and experience required for acceptance to the medical staff. If not, the physician simply does not apply.

Prior to 1992, there was a lack of clarity about whether the HCQIA requires reporting to the NPDB when an applicant does not meet the threshold criteria. The HCQIA specifies that physicians who are denied privileges by the board based on clinical competence must be reported to the NPDB. There is no exception for submitting an application for initial appointment. A literal reading of the reporting requirement would mandate submission of a report to the NPDB if a physician applied for medical staff membership but was denied because he or she did not have sufficient clinical experience to meet the facility's eligibility criteria. Many facilities saw the preapplication process as a way to avoid triggering a reporting duty. The 1992 *NPDB Guidebook Supplement*, however, states that a denial of privileges based on threshold eligibility requirements is not reportable even if the criterion is quality related.

INITIAL APPLICATION

Q.5:7 For what does an applicant to the medical staff apply?

The applicant seeks medical staff membership, which includes designation of a specific category of medical staff membership, assignment to a particular service or department, and delineation of clinical privileges, indicating which medical procedures the practitioner may perform at the hospital.

Q.5:8 Why is the design of the application form important?

The purpose of the application form is to gather sufficient information upon which to make a valid decision regarding the applicant's eligibility for membership. The questions should be clearly stated and unambiguous so there is no misunderstanding about what information is being elicited.

Care should be taken that the questions do not violate state or federal law. State human rights, employment laws, and credentialing laws, if any, must be taken into account, as well as federal civil rights laws, such as the ADA.

A well-designed form should require the applicant's signed consent to obtain information and should contain a release of liability.

The form must meet Joint Commission requirements as well. Joint Commission surveyors will check the application form for compliance with the standards.

Q.5:9 How is the "delineation of privileges" form structured?

The purpose of the "delineation of privileges" form is to ascertain what procedures the applicant is seeking to perform at the facility. This form can be structured in many different ways.

The form may actually list all of the procedures the applicant may potentially perform and request the applicant to indicate the procedures he or she wishes to perform at the facility.

The form may separate procedures into various levels based on complexity. The applicant may apply for privileges for all procedures in levels 1 and 2, for example. Or the form may allow the applicant to request privileges to perform all procedures in levels 1 and 2 and only specific procedures in levels 3 and 4.

The form may use specialty designations in which privileges are defined by board certification in particular specialties or subspecialties. If an applicant is granted privileges based on specialty designation, the practitioner may be entitled to perform a basic package of procedures identified by CPT or ICD–9 codes, as determined by the department, credentials committee or executive committee, and the board. Individuals who are not board-certified may be required to show competence to perform such procedures by other evidence.

The form may use a categorical approach in which procedures are defined in terms of hierarchy of levels based on disease groupings. The form may further categorize based on a physician's level of competence or experience.

However the form is structured, the applicant is required to provide evidence of competence to perform the procedures for which privileges are requested. The information submitted by the applicant concerning relevant training or number of procedures performed and complication rates will be evaluated against the criteria recommended by the medical staff and approved by the governing board.

Q.5:10 What kind of information is requested in the application for appointment to the medical staff and delineation of privileges for a physician?

According to the Joint Commission, professional criteria used to evaluate candidates for medical staff membership or delineated clinical privileges must pertain to at least evidence of current licensure, relevant training and experience, current competence, and health status. [MS 2.4.1.3 (1994)]

The Joint Commission standards require that the medical staff bylaws, rules and regulations, or policies define the information each applicant for appointment or reappointment to the medical staff and initial or renewed/revised clinical privileges must provide. The information must include at least:

- previously successful or currently pending challenges to licensure or registration or the voluntary relinquishment of such licensure or registration
- voluntary or involuntary termination of medical staff membership or voluntary or involuntary limitation, reduction, or loss of clinical privileges at another hospital
- involvement in a professional liability action under circumstances specified in the medical staff bylaws, rules and regulations, and policies (at least final judgments or settlements involving the individual) [MS 2.5 (1994)]

The completed form should contain

- a statement that the applicant has received or has had access to a copy of the bylaws, rules, and regulations
- the applicant's agreement to abide by the provisions of the bylaws, rules, and regulations if he or she is granted membership
- detailed information concerning the applicant's qualifications, including training, licensure, and related experience
- a statement of the staff category, service, and clinical privileges for which the applicant wishes to be considered
- a listing of personal and professional references
- information concerning professional discipline taken or pending against the applicant
- the applicant's agreement to exhaust internal administrative remedies before litigating in the event an adverse ruling is made
- consent directed to third parties authorizing them to release information to the hospital

It should be made clear to the applicant that he or she has signified willingness to be interviewed by members of the medical staff, have references and previous and current affiliations at other hospitals checked, and have inquiries made into physical and mental health and professional qualifications.

The form should contain a release of liability to those gathering, sending, and acting on information regarding the application if such release is allowable under state law.

Q.5:11 What kind of questions should be asked about licensure?

In addition to questions regarding current licensure in the state where the facility is located, the hospital may ask if the applicant is licensed in any other state, whether any action has been taken against his or her license in any jurisdiction, including revocation, suspension, censure, fines, practice restriction or any other type of discipline, and whether the practitioner has ever voluntarily surrendered a license. The form should also inquire about Drug Enforcement Agency (DEA) certification and whether it has ever been revoked.

Q.5:12 What kind of questions should be asked regarding insurance?

Questions regarding insurance generally include coverage amount, kind of coverage (tail, claims made, occurrence), and carrier. Additional questions a hospital may also want to ask are whether the practitioner's malpractice insurance has ever been terminated by the action of the insurance coverage and whether there are limitations in the scope of coverage regarding any practices or procedures.

Q.5:13 What kind of questions should be asked regarding affiliations with other facilities?

The applicant is generally asked to identify the names and addresses of other facilities where he or she holds privileges at the present time, including hospitals, nursing homes, home care agencies, and similar facilities, and may inquire about past affiliations as well. The facility may also inquire as to what privileges the applicant holds at each location.

The hospital may ask applicants to document that they have conformed with the bylaws rules and regulations of other facilities with which they have been associated. This type of information is vital to an adequate evaluation of the applicant, and it is fair to put the burden on the applicant to prove that he or she is able to comply with a facility's bylaws and regulations.

Q.5:14 Are there legal problems with questions regarding health status?

The Joint Commission specifies that the medical staff bylaws must require that applicants for appointment and reappointment submit information on current health status. [MS 2.4.1.3 (1994)] The ADA, on the other hand, prohibits pre-employment inquiries concerning an applicant's medical condition. [42 U.S.C. §12112 (d)(2)] The Joint Commission has attempted to resolve the issue in a scoring guideline, noting that it "has and will absolutely construe [the accreditation standards] in such a manner as not to be inconsistent with hospital efforts to comply with the ADA." (*Accreditation Manual for Hospitals, Scoring Guidelines, Medical Staff,* The Joint Commission on Accreditation of Healthcare Organizations. Oakbrook, IL, 1994, 10)

Q.5:15 What questions may an employer ask under the ADA?

On May 19, 1994, the ADA Division of the Office of Legal Counsel released a guidance that sets forth the EEOC's position on whether various disability-related pre-employment inquiries comply with the ADA. The following questions are inquiries that are not disability-related and are, therefore, legal:

- Can you perform the functions of this job (essential and/or marginal) with or without reasonable accommodation?

- Please describe/demonstrate how you would perform these functions (essential and/or marginal).
- Do you have a cold? Have you ever tried Tylenol for fever? How did you break your leg?
- Can you meet the attendance requirements of this job? How many days did you take leave last year?
- Do you illegally use drugs? Have you used illegal drugs in the last two years?
- Do you have the required licenses to perform this job?
- How much do you weigh? How tall are you? Do you regularly eat three meals per day?

[EEOC: Enforcement Guidance on Pre-Employment Inquiries Under the Americans With Disabilities Act, May 19, 1994]

Q.5:16 What questions are illegal under the ADA?

On May 19, 1994, the ADA Division of the Office of Legal Counsel released a guidance that sets forth the EEOC's position on whether various disability-related pre-employment inquiries comply with the ADA. The guidance identifies the following questions as disability-related and, therefore, illegal:

- Do you have AIDS? Do you have asthma?
- Do you have a disability that would interfere with your ability to perform the job?
- How many days were you sick last year?
- Have you ever filed for workers' compensation? Have you ever been injured on the job?
- How much alcohol do you drink each week? Have you ever been treated for alcohol problems?
- Have you ever been treated for mental health problems?
- What prescription drugs are you currently taking?

[EEOC: Enforcement Guidance on Pre-Employment Inquiries Under the Americans With Disabilities Act, May 19, 1994]

Q.5:17 Are there cases concerning permissible questions for physicians under the ADA?

A 1993 case involving an application form for a medical license is interesting in this context even though the case was grounded on Title II of the ADA, which prohibits public entities from discriminating against disabled persons in the granting of licenses. A federal court in New Jersey held that license applications that contain questions regarding mental illness and substance abuse probably violate the ADA. The initial and renewal medical license application forms contained questions such as "Are you now or have you been dependent on alcohol or drugs?" An applicant who answered "yes" to any of the questions was required to explain the circumstances in detail. In addition, the renewal application stated that the failure to answer any question, in part or whole, was grounds for denial. [*The Medical Society of New Jersey v. Jacobs*, No. 93-3670 (D.N.J. Oct. 5, 1993)]

The court pointed out that because the questions were so broadly worded, the vast majority of applicants who answered "yes" were nonetheless qualified individuals with disabilities. The court ruled, however, that the questions themselves were not discriminatory. Rather, it was the extra investigation of qualified applicants who answer "yes" that constituted discrimination. Requiring further explanation and investigation of the circumstances surrounding a "yes" answer imposed extra burdens on qualified disabled persons who were trying to obtain or renew medical licenses, which violates the ADA, the court ruled. While the court acknowledged that it is necessary to inquire into an applicant's fitness, there are many other ways of doing so, including the use of references and checking with the NPDB.

Q.5:18 Should the application form state that individuals involved in the credentialing process are entitled to absolute immunity from suit?

Such language should be included on the application form. Some state laws, for example, the law in Illinois, specifically grant absolute immunity to those involved in credentialing process. Other states may grant immunity only to decisions reached in good faith, which is a form of limited immunity. Nonetheless, including absolute immunity language on the application form and in the bylaws or other credentialing policies bolsters the argument that the applicant willingly agreed to grant the participants absolute immunity.

The Joint Commission approves the use of such hold-harmless or immunity statements [MS 2.11.3 (1994)], and their use has been upheld by several courts. [See *Stitzel v. York Mem. Osteopathic Hosp.*, 754 F. Supp. 1061 (M.D. Pa. 1991).]

Q.5:19 What if the application is not complete when submitted?

Because the hospital is required to process so many applications and the process is both time-consuming and costly, the hospital bylaws or credentialing policy should put the burden on the applicant to provide a complete application. The bylaws should define what constitutes a complete application (The Joint Commission requires that the bylaws define complete application) and indicate that unresolved questions regarding an applicant render an application incomplete. The definition of a complete application can state that an application is complete only when all verifying information is received. Applicants should be notified in writing that no application will be processed until the application is complete.

The importance of submitting nothing less than a complete and accurate application form was illustrated by a New York case in which a physician who gave inaccurate responses to questions on separate applications for medical staff privileges at two hospitals had his medical license suspended and was required to perform 50 hours of public service. A hospital suspended and later terminated the physician's admitting privileges because he had admitted, in violation of hospital rules, several patients when he was not carrying medical malpractice insurance. Meanwhile, the physician applied for reappointment to the medical staff of another hospital and indicated on the reappointment application that his privileges had never been suspended or revoked. He gained temporary privileges at the second hospital, but shortly thereafter, those privileges were terminated because he did not have malpractice insurance when he admitted patients. The following month, the physician applied for privileges at a third hospital. He acknowledged that his privileges had not been renewed at the first hospital but neglected to mention the nonrenewal of his privileges at the second facility.

A hearing committee of the State Board of Professional Medical Conduct found the physician guilty of practicing his profession fraudulently and committing unprofessional conduct. The penalty was 100 hours of public service and suspension of his license for a year, with execution stayed. A New York court reduced the public service penalty to 50 hours but otherwise upheld the decision.

The bylaws should make it clear that not only does the applicant have the burden of submitting a complete application but the burden of establishing that he or she should be granted membership and privileges. If information is not forthcoming, or if questions are not adequately resolved, appointment will be denied.

Q.5:20 What if the information is not received within a reasonable time period?

The credentialing policy should indicate the maximum time frame for accepting information for an application before the actual credentialing process begins. If the application is not completed within six months, for example, including all references, evidence of licensure, and other required information, the hospital may require resubmission to avoid reliance on stale information. To avoid a situation in which the applicant believes the application is complete and is being processed when in reality information is missing and the application process has therefore not begun, administrative personnel should notify the applicant in writing that the application is on hold and indicate the reason. The applicant should be informed of the deadline for submitting the appropriate information to avoid having to resubmit all information.

Q.5:21 Is there a particular time frame for processing applications?

The medical staff bylaws generally indicate the applicable time limits. The bylaws can specify that processing will not begin until all verifying information is received. The Joint Commission requires that applications be processed within a reasonable time. Some specific time limits are dictated by the requirements of the HCQIA. In addition, state law may impose certain time requirements. The District of Columbia health care licensure statute, for example, mandates that a facility grant or deny an application for membership or privileges within 120 calendar days. [D.C. Code 1981 §32-1307 (1993)]

Q.5:22 What are the consequences if the applicant falsifies information on the application form?

Knowingly withholding information or providing false or fraudulent information on the application form is sufficient to warrant denying the physician privileges, and should be stated on the application form itself. Several courts have upheld the denial of privileges based on incomplete or false information on applications. [See *Garrison v. Board of Trustees*, 795 P.2d 190 (Wyo. 1990); *Pariser v. Christian Health Care Systems Inc.* 681 F. Supp. 1381 (E.D. Mo. 1988).]

VERIFICATION

Q.5:23 Who has the duty to verify the information on the application?

The hospital has the legal duty to evaluate and monitor the competence of physicians granted membership and privileges. An important aspect of this duty is to verify the information it initially receives from an applicant.

Q.5:24 What information must be verified?

Verification of four major areas must be obtained: current licensure, relevant training and experience, competence, and health status.

The Joint Commission requires hospitals to verify information from primary sources, when possible, about the applicant's licensure, training, experience, and current competence. [MS 2.4.1.3.1 (1994)]

Q.5:25 How is licensure, education, and training verified?

The Joint Commission indicates that the following primary sources should be contacted:

- to confirm licensure, the state medical licensing board
- to confirm graduation from medical school, the applicant's medical school
- to confirm satisfactory completion of postgraduate training, the chief of the applicant's residency program

These items should be verified in writing. [See *Medical Staff Credentialing: Questions and Answers About the Joint Commission's Standards*, The Joint Commission on Accreditation of Healthcare Organizations. Oakbrook, IL, 1993, 15.]

Q.5:26 How is competency verified for initial appointment and privileging?

Current competence can be verified through contacting other facilities, training programs, and peer references, and obtaining letters or completed forms from individuals who are personally knowledgeable about the practitioner's performance. This written documentation should indicate the applicant's competence in the areas for which he or she seeks privileges.

Q.5:27 How is current health status verified?

According to the Joint Commission, for initial application, health status can be verified by the director of a training program, the chief of services or chief of staff at another hospital where the applicant holds privileges, or a currently licensed physician designated by the hospital. [See *Medical Staff Credentialing: Questions and Answers About the Joint Commission's Standards*, The Joint Commission on Accreditation of Healthcare Organizations. Oakbrook, IL, 1993, 19.]

Q.5:28 What other information should be verified from primary sources?

Other information that should be verified in writing from primary sources includes specialty board statutes, professional liability insurance coverage, other health care facility affiliations, professional references, and the NPDB report.

Q.5:29 What can be done if a reference refuses to put adverse information in writing?

A CEO or a medical staff leader may be more willing to divulge negative information in a telephone conversation or during a personal visit from a representative of the facility seeking to verify an applicant's credentials. If such methods are used, the person eliciting the information should take careful notes and should have the notes verified by the person divulging the information. If possible, the person being interviewed should sign the notes. This is important because the applicant may be rejected on the basis of such adverse recommendations, and the hospital will need evidence that the adverse recommendation actually took place.

It may help to remind the reluctant reference that applicants sign releases permitting references to truthfully divulge information. In addition, many state peer review laws provide immunity for those who participate in the peer review process.

Q.5:30 What is the National Practitioner Data Bank?

The National Practitioner Data Bank (NPDB) was mandated by the HCQIA of 1986. [42 U.S.C. §§11101–11152] It is a database that contains adverse information regarding certain health care practitioners. The intent of the NPDB was to prevent incompetent practitioners from moving from state to state without detection.

The provisions regarding the NPDB contain both reporting and inquiry requirements.

Q.5:31 What are the reporting requirements of the NPDB?

Health care entities must report certain information to the NPDB through their state licensing boards. Health care entities include hospitals or other entities that provide health care services and engage in professional review activity through a formal peer review process for the purpose of furthering quality health care. Health care entities must report any professional review action that adversely affects the clinical privileges of a physician or dentist for a period of longer than 30 days. "Professional review action" means an action or recommendation of a health care entity:

- taken in the course of professional review activity, defined as an activity of a health care entity to determine whether a physician, dentist, or other health care practitioner may have clinical privileges with respect to, or membership in, the entity; to determine the scope or conditions of such privileges or membership; or to change or modify such privileges or membership;
- based on the professional competence or professional conduct of an individual physician, dentist, or other health care practitioner, which affects or could affect adversely the health or welfare of a patient; and

- that adversely affects or may adversely affect the practitioner's clinical privileges or membership in a professional society. "Adversely affects" means reducing, restricting, suspending, revoking, denying clinical privileges in or membership in a health care entity. [42 U.S.C. §11151 (9)]

Q.5:32 When must a summary suspension be reported?

A summary suspension must be reported if it is reviewed, confirmed, modified, or revised by an authorized health care entity committee, lasts for more than 30 days, and is based on professional competence. A suspension imposed by an individual is not reportable until a professional review action takes place. Health care entities must also report if a practitioner surrenders clinical privileges or any restriction of privileges while the practitioner is under investigation by the health care entity for possible incompetence or improper professional conduct in return for not conducting such an investigation or proceeding. [42 U.S.C. §11133]

Q.5:33 Are there special reporting requirements for self-insured health care entities?

In addition to adverse actions affecting clinical privileges, a health care entity that is also a self-insurer must report medical malpractice payments on behalf of health care practitioners within one month of the payment. [42 U.S.C. §§11131, 11134] Payments that must be reported include those in satisfaction of a legal judgment as well as those made under a settlement or partial settlement agreement. A health care entity that fails to report such payments may be fined up to $10,000 for each failure. [42 U.S.C. §11131]

Q.5:34 What need not be reported to the NPDB?

Hospitals need not report actions that are primarily based on a physician's, dentist's, or other health care practitioner's association, or lack of association, with a professional society or association; fees, advertising or other competitive acts intended to solicit or retain business; participation in prepaid group health plans, salaried employment, or any other manner of delivering health services; association with a member or members of a particular class of health care practitioner or professional; or any other matter that does not relate to the competence or professional conduct of the health care practitioner. [42 U.S.C. §11151]

Q.5:35 When must NPDB reports be made?

Reports of adverse actions on clinical privileges must be made within one month of the action. Health care entities must submit an adverse action report to the state medical or dental board within 15 days of the action being taken. The state boards are responsible for submitting all reports directly to the data bank and the appropriate licensing board, if necessary, within 15 days from the date of its receipt. Any revision to the action must be reported within 15 days of the revision. [45 C.F. R. §60.6 (b)]

Note that the reporting requirement refers to final actions only. Therefore, if the time to appeal an action has not expired, the action is not yet final. In addition, if an appeal is requested the action does not become final until appeal measures are exhausted in most cases.

If a health care entity fails to report adverse actions on clinical privileges, after appropriate hearings, the Department of Health and Human Services (DHHS) will publish the name of the health care entity in the federal register and the immunity provisions of the HCQIA will not apply to professional review activities that occur during the three-year period beginning 30 days after the date of publication. [42 U.S.C. §§11134, 11111 (b)].

Q.5:36 What kind of practitioners are included in the NPDB?

The health care professionals included in the NPDB are doctors of medicine and osteopathy, dentists, and other individuals licensed or otherwise authorized by a state to provide health care services. [Department of Health and Human Services, *National Practitioner Data Bank Guidebook*, Supplement, 1992] Although the act requires only the reporting of adverse professional review actions against physicians and dentists except in medical malpractice cases, HHS has elected to include any voluntarily reported information regarding other licensed health care practitioners in the NPDB. [42 U.S.C. §11133] Whether certain health care practitioners are included within the definition varies by state law. Examples of the type of health care practitioner that might be included are optometrists, pharmacists, physical therapists, respiratory therapists, nurse anesthetists, registered nurses, medical technologists, home health aides, and dietitians. (See *NPDB Guidebook* for more extensive, though not exhaustive listing.)

Q.5:37 Is information reported to the NPDB considered confidential?

Information reported to the NPDB is confidential and may not be disclosed, except in connection with peer review and as necessary to carry out the requirements of HCQIA. [42 U.S.C. §11137(b)] Entities that receive information directly from the NPDB may disclose it to others only for the purpose of professional review activity within the entity. According to federal regulations, those who receive NPDB information indirectly may use the information only for the purpose for which it was provided, presumably professional peer review activity. [45 C.F.R. §60.13; *Guidebook Supplement* 21 (1992) at 7] Further, an attorney who receives information from the NPDB in connection with a malpractice suit may use the information only within the context of that particular suit. HCQIA confidentiality provisions do not protect the original documents from which the reported information was obtained, however, and do not prevent disclosure otherwise authorized by state law. To protect the confidentiality of the information, a civil money penalty of up to $10,000 for each violation may be assessed against any person or entity wrongfully disclosing confidential information. [42 U.S.C. §11137(b)]

A practitioner who is reported receives a copy of the report and an opportunity to submit comments that will subsequently be sent out with the report when the data bank is queried.

A federal trial court has held that HCQIA's confidentiality protections do not prevent a physician suing a hospital on antitrust grounds from obtaining peer review records. The court ruled that because Congress did not intend to "hide" antitrust violations, the limited privilege is not applicable when a physician files an antitrust claim. [*Pagano v. Oroville Hospital*, 145 F.R.D. 683 (E.D. Cal. 1993)]

Q.5:38 What are the NPDB inquiry requirements?

A health care entity must query the NPDB to obtain information regarding the standing of a physician, dentist, or other health care practitioner when the individual applies for a position on the medical staff (courtesy or otherwise) or for clinical privileges at the hospital. Information must also be requested every two years at the time of reappointment of these practitioners.

Q.5:39 Who may request information from the NPDB?

A hospital may request information concerning a physician, dentist, or other health care practitioner who is a member of the medical staff having clinical privileges at the hospital at any time. Other health care entities may request information if they have established an employment or affiliation relationship with a physician, dentist, or other health care practitioner or if they may establish such a relationship. Health care entities may also request information if a practitioner has applied for clinical privileges or appointment to the medical staff or in connection with a professional review activity. [45 C.F.R. §60.11]

An attorney or individual representing himself or herself who has filed a medical malpractice action in a state or federal court or other adjudicative body against a hospital and who requests information regarding a specific physician, dentist, or other health care practitioner who is also named in the action or claim may request information from the NPDB. This information will be disclosed only on submission of evidence that the hospital failed to request information from the NPDB as required under HCQIA and may be used solely with respect to litigation resulting from the action or claim against the hospital. [45 C.F.R. §60.11]

Q.5:40 Can a hospital rely on the information it receives from the NPDB?

A hospital may rely on the information provided by the NPDB and will not be held liable for such reliance unless the hospital has knowledge that the information provided was false. [42 U.S.C. §11135]

Q.5:41 What is the legal effect if the hospital does not query the NPDB?

A hospital that does not request information required by HCQIA is presumed to have knowledge of any information reported to the NPDB concerning a particular physician, dentist, or other practitioner. A hospital has a corporate duty to properly credential practitioners. Failure to do so could result in hospital liability.

Q.5:42 Is the use of outside credentials verification services acceptable?

There are external credentials verification services that provide hospitals and other health care entities with credentialing information. Some county medical societies, for example, conduct primary source verification.

The hospital retains the legal responsibility to verify the information whether it is done through in-house personnel or through an outside organization. Therefore, if a hospital uses an outside organization for this process, it should be assured of its effectiveness.

As long as such services provide information from primary sources and provide copies to the hospital, the use of credentials verification services meets Joint Commission standards.

Q.5:43 What other data banks can be consulted?

The Federation of State Medical Boards operates a Physician Board Action Data Bank that can reveal valuable credentialing information. The federation is a private organization whose mission is to assist in credentialing matters. All of the state medical boards as well as the Armed Forces, Veterans Administration (VA), and

Department of Health and Human Services (DHHS), provide information to the data bank concerning MDs, DOs, and PAs.

The Physician Board Action Data Bank does not include information on medical malpractice. It does contain information regarding disciplinary actions, such as Medicare/Medicaid fraud sanctions, information on impaired physicians who have been disciplined, and formal actions taken against a practitioner's license. For example, felony convictions are included if the state board decided to take action against the practitioner's license but are not included if the board decided not to take such action. The data base also contains nondisciplinary information that may be valuable in the credentialing process. For example, it reports voluntary surrender of a license, and lost licenses (requests for duplicate licenses). These are matters that would need to be investigated further.

A practitioner who is reported in the data bank can get a copy of his or her file. Hospitals, MCOs, and credentialing agencies can access the data bank if the entity has a contract with the federation and submits a release form from the practitioners whose credentials they are checking.

Q.5:44 Is there potential liability attached to verifying information?

There is a potential for liability, although it is remote. It is possible that the process of verifying information could give rise to charges of breach of confidentiality or defamation. To guard against such charges, the person verifying the information should ensure that the proper releases are signed and that everything is properly documented.

EVALUATION

Q.5:45 Who reviews the application after the information is verified?

After the application is complete and the necessary attachments are obtained, the file is reviewed by the department chair, who makes recommendations regarding the delineation of privileges. If the department chair discovers incomplete or misleading information, he or she can request further clarification. The application is then reviewed by the credentials committee, which recommends approval or denial of the application. The medical executive committee then reviews the application and the recommendations and makes its own recommendation for approval or denial. The executive committee's recommendation is forwarded to the governing body, which makes the final decision.

Q.5:46 Can the governing board reject the recommendation of the executive committee?

Yes, the governing board is not to function as a rubber stamp, or it would not legitimately be making the final decision. In one case, a medical staff executive committee sued the board for rejecting its recommendation to suspend a medical staff member's privileges and reassign the physician to a lower category of the medical staff. The court ruled that the medical staff executive committee had no standing to sue the board because the committee was a creation of the governing board, answerable to the governing board and acting as an arm of the board. [*Ad Hoc Executive Committee v. Runyan,* 716 P.2d 465 (Col. 1986)]

Q.5:47 Do numerous outstanding lawsuits against an applicant require that the application be rejected?

Numerous outstanding lawsuits do not indicate that the application should automatically be rejected but do raise a red flag indicating the need for further investigation. It could be that the practitioner treats high-risk patients and can provide a satisfactory explanation for the large number of outstanding lawsuits. In addition, practitioners from some specialties, such as radiology and pathology, are routinely included in lawsuits and are eventually dismissed.

Q.5:48 What if the appointment is different than requested?

The board may approve the applicant's admission to the medical staff but deny specific privileges that it determines the applicant is not qualified to hold. In that case, the denial of privileges must be reported to the NPDB because the denial of privileges was based on clinical competence. In addition, the denial of privileges may trigger the right to a hearing, depending on the hospital's bylaws or fair hearing plan and state law.

The board may avoid the necessity of reporting to the NPDB while at the same time protecting patient safety by attaching some requirements to the granting of the requested privileges. For example, the board may require additional training or a specified schedule permitting the physician to perform the procedure with supervision or other conditions.

Q.5:49 Must a hospital explain its reasons for denial?

The physician should be notified in writing of the denial and should be given the reasons for such denial. HCQIA requires that specific reasons be given for denial. Case law may also indicate that such notice is necessary. In a 1992 case, for example, the Supreme Court of Alaska ruled that a private hospital had violated a physician's due process rights by denying his application for staff privileges without an adequate explanation. After oral interviews with two physicians, the applicant was informed that his request for staff privileges was denied because only physicians who can document their background, experience, training, and competence were eligible for membership. There was no indication of how he fell short of those requirements. The physician appealed the denial, but both an ad hoc committee and an appellate review committee affirmed the denial.

The court ruled that the hospital did not give the physician proper notice of the reason his application was denied and, therefore, violated due process. Criteria for granting or denying privileges should not be vague and ambiguous, the court reasoned, and should be applied objectively. Basic principles of due process require that when a hospital denies an application, it must notify the applicant of the specific criteria that were determinative and how the applicant failed to meet the hospital's standards with regard to those criteria. The court clarified that its ruling does not mean that an oral examination may not be given. However, if the answers to the oral examination are used to deny an application for privileges, the hospital must establish criteria for determining whether the applicant passed the examination and must have a process so that an applicant can challenge the conduct of the examination and the hospital's evaluation of the answers. [*Kiester v. Humana Hospital Alaska, Inc.* 843 P.2d 1219 (Alaska 1992)]

Q.5:50 Is a practitioner entitled to a hearing upon denial of an application?

Whether or not the physician is entitled to a hearing upon denial depends on the reason for the denial as well as on the hospital's bylaws. For example, if the application for membership was denied because the physician's license has lapsed or because the hospital has an exclusive contract with a group and, therefore, is not accepting applications for medical staff membership in a particular specialty, a hearing would serve no purpose.

The Joint Commission requires that there be mechanisms that include a fair hearing and appeal process for addressing adverse decisions for the applicant. [MS 2.12.1 (1994)] Some state statutes or regulations govern the legal requirements necessary when an applicant is denied. Such laws generally require notice and documentation supporting the rejection.

The courts in some states have held that procedural due process rights are available to applicants for membership on the medical staff, and when procedures are set forth in hospital or medical staff documents, they have a right to invoke the hospital's fair hearing procedure at the "threshold" of medical staff appointment. [See *Cohen v. Cook County*, 677 F. Supp. 547 (N.D. Ill. 1988).] In states where there have not been similar rulings, a hospital may decide and incorporate into its bylaws or fair hearing plan that hearing rights are not available to practitioners who are not members of the medical staff. The adverse side of this policy decision is that if the practitioner has no hospital forum in which to challenge the denial, that practitioner may decide to challenge the denial in court.

If the application is denied for reasons relating to competence, the denial must be reported to the NPDB.

REAPPOINTMENT

Q.5:51 How often are practitioners reappointed to the medical staff?

The reappointment process takes place for each practitioner at least once every two years. This is in accordance with the requirements of the Joint Commission, NCQA, and NPDB, state law, and Medicare Conditions of Participation.

Q.5:52 How does the reappointment process differ from the initial appointment process?

The initial appointment process focuses on the practitioner's education, training, and other professional history before obtaining privileges at the institution. The information needed to verify the practitioner's credentials comes from outside sources. The reappointment process focuses on the practitioner's professional behavior and competence while functioning at the institution. While some outside sources are still contacted to verify certain information, much of the information that is required for reappointment can be obtained from internal sources, such as quality assurance professionals, medical records staff, risk managers, and legal staff, as well as other practitioners, such as the department chair.

Q.5:53 What kind of information can be gathered from in-house sources for use in reappointment?

There are many sources of information that can be evaluated, including drug utilization reports from pharmacy and therapeutics committee; surgical case review and other outcome data; infection control reports; blood utilization reviews; diagnostic utilization reviews; morbidity and mortality statistics; incident reports or unusual occurrence reports; and risk management reports.

For MCOs, the reappointment process should include review of data from member complaints and member satisfaction surveys.

Q.5:54 What are the criteria used to evaluate a candidate for reappointment?

The Joint Commission specifies that reappointment to the medical staff or renewal/revision of clinical privileges should be based on information concerning the individual's professional performance, judgment, and clinical or technical skills, as indicated in part by the results of quality assessment and improvement activities. [MS 2.7 (1994)] According to the Joint Commission, "professional performance" and "clinical and/or technical skills" are objective determinations based on the results of peer review, monitoring and evaluation activities including review of surgical and other invasive procedures, blood usage review, and drug usage and other evaluations. "Professional performance" can also include adherence to medical staff bylaws, rules and regulations, and policies. "Judgment" is a subjective determination, but it is derived from information from peer review and other evaluations." [See *Medical Staff Credentialing: Questions and Answers about the Joint Commission's Standards*, The Joint Commission on Accreditation of Healthcare Organizations. Oakbrook, IL, 1993, 21.]

Q.5:55 Can continuing education be used as a criterion in the reappointment process?

The Joint Commission's standards indicate that an individual's participation in continuing education should be considered at the time of reappointment and/or renewal or revision of clinical privileges. [MS 6.2.2 (1994)] The requirements for continuing education should be documented and available to practitioners. The reappointment form should ask what kind of continuing education programs the applicant has participated in and how many hours of Continuing Medical Education (CME) have been completed since the last appointment.

Q.5:56 Can peer review recommendations be used as a criterion in the reappointment process?

The Joint Commission's standards state that peer recommendations should be part of the basis for the development of recommendations for reappointment to the staff and renewal/revision of clinical privileges. [MS 2.8 (1994)]

Q.5:57 What kind of questions are asked at the time of reappointment?

The applicant for reappointment should complete a form that confirms or updates the information contained in the credentialing file, such as demographic information, current status and all changes in licensure or registration, liability coverage, and specialty board certification. In addition, the form should pose questions regarding such matters as denial or revocation of membership or participation status at other health care entities and professional societies, voluntary or involuntary limitation or revocation of privileges at other health care entities, information regarding settlements, judgments, and pending professional liability cases, and information regarding health status. The NPDB must also be queried.

Q.5:58 Who reviews the application for reappointment?

The application form and accompanying profile information should be reviewed by the appropriate clinical department chairperson, the credentials committee, the medical executive committee, and the governing body.

Q.5:59 How can the clinical competence of a low-volume or a no-volume physician, such as a physician on the courtesy staff, be evaluated?

Medical staff services personnel can identify hospitals where the physician is active, obtain the physician's written consent for these facilities to release requested information, and send the facilities a copy of the release along with a questionnaire form. The form should explain that the physician is in the reappointment process and that the hospital requires letters of clinical competency from other hospitals where the physician holds staff membership. The form should contain questions that are normally asked during the reappointment process. It should be signed by the appropriate department chair and sent or faxed back to the inquiring hospital's medical staff office.

Q.5:60 What are the typical steps in the reappointment process?

1. Ninety days prior to the membership expiration date, the medical staff services:
   - sends a reappointment application to the practitioner, including the deadline for receipt
   - notifies the quality assurance department of the need for a practitioner clinical profile and the date needed
   - submits the name of the practitioner being reappointed to the National Practitioner Data Bank and requests information
2. Sixty days prior to the expiration date, the practitioner returns the completed application form. The quality assurance department forwards the profile to medical staff services.
3. Medical staff services verifies the information on the completed application and sends the application, administrative data, NPDB information, clinical profile, privilege delineation request form, and verification from other facilities (in the case of a practitioner relatively inactive at the hospital) to the department chairperson for review.
4. The department chairperson reviews the profile and all supporting information, comments on the practitioner's health status, and sends a written recommendation for privilege delineation and reappointment to the credentials committee.
5. The credentials committee reviews all information and the department chairperson's recommendation and submits its recommendation to the executive committee.
6. The executive committee reviews the previous recommendations, makes its own recommendation, and then forwards it to the governing body. (If an adverse recommendation is made, the applicant must be offered due process.)

7. The governing body takes final action.
8. The applicant is notified of the governing body's decision.

[Orsund-Gassiot and Lindsey, *Handbook of Medical Staff Management*, "The Credentials Process." F.C. Dimond, Jr., Gaithersburg, MD: Aspen Publishers, Inc. 1990, Exhibit 8-5; 128]

Q.5:61 Have there been any recent cases regarding the question of corporate negligence for negligent renewal of medical staff privileges?

In a 1993 case, a patient who suffered brain damage from oxygen deprivation charged that a hospital was liable under the theory of corporate negligence because it had failed to exercise reasonable care in renewing the staff privileges of the physician who had refused to perform a tracheostomy on her. The patient's care was delayed while another physician who would perform the procedure was located. The patient contended that the hospital had been negligent in renewing the physician's privileges to perform tracheostomies, arguing that if the hospital had investigated the physician's clinical activities, it would have discovered that he had not performed a tracheostomy in recent years. The patient claimed that the hospital could, therefore, have reasonably inferred that the physician might be incapable of or might refuse to perform a tracheostomy.

The hospital's process of reappointing staff physicians revolved around the honor system in which applicants were expected to inform the hospital if they no longer performed any of the listed procedures. The patient contended that this process did not conform with the bylaws, which provided that "Biennial re-appointment shall follow an appraisal of clinical activity, professional performance an[d] a re-assessment of the extent of clinical privileges to be granted."

A jury had returned a verdict for the patient of over 4 million dollars. The Supreme Court of Rhode Island, however, reversed that decision, directing a verdict for the hospital. On the issue of corporate negligence, the court held that the patient had to show that the hospital would have discovered the physician's reluctance or inability to perform tracheostomies if it had performed the recommended and customary investigation into his previous clinical activities. The court concluded that the hospital had not done so. There was no proof that further investigation into the physician's clinical activities would have affected the renewal of his privileges. The court noted that there had been no complaints or adverse actions taken against the physician and that he had not refused to perform the procedure in the past. The court reasoned that physicians are trained to do many procedures that they are not frequently called on to perform. Simply because a physician has not performed a procedure for a particular period of time does not support the inference that he or she is incapable of doing so, the court concluded. [*Rodrigues v. Miriam Hospital*, 623 A.2d 456 (R.I. 1993)]

6

Termination, Suspension, or Restriction of Privileges

Q.6:1 What are the different degrees of discipline that might be imposed on a medical staff member?

The medical staff bylaws should delineate the various possible degrees of discipline that may be imposed by the hospital. It is important that the medical staff bylaws indicate who has the authority to invoke discipline "or other action deemed appropriate by the board," and some general criteria for determining the degree of severity of the sanction.

The most serious action a governing board can take against a medical staff member is termination of staff membership. Termination can be accomplished by the governing board's withdrawal of medical staff membership or by failure to reappoint under bylaws requiring periodic reappointment.

Temporary suspension may be total or partial. It may involve suspension of all privileges, or may involve only certain specified privileges. The suspension is usually invoked as a protective device in the interest of patient safety.

Privilege reduction may result from a practitioner's incompetence or because the practitioner has not had the opportunity to perform those procedures that are the subject of the reduction. Privileges may also be reduced for nondisciplinary reasons, such as the facility's inability to provide adequate equipment or the facility's decision to discontinue certain services.

A staff member may be placed on probation for a stated period or until certain deficiencies in performance are corrected. Probation may be imposed due to clinical shortcomings or other behavior not related to patient care that the medical staff or governing body finds improper and not in the best interest of the institution or its patients.

Supervision by other medical staff members may result from clinical deficiencies or suspected inadequacies that may be resolved by the presence of another practitioner.

Delay in advancement from the associate staff to the active medical staff may result from clinical inadequacies or as a disciplinary device in response to poor behavior. If the hospital's bylaws require advancement from associate to active staff within a specified time or staff membership is terminated, a delay in advancement may be tantamount to termination, and the affected practitioner may demand due process rights.

Letters containing reprimands, admonitions, and warnings to practitioners are a common disciplinary device for minor infractions of hospital rules. Continued violations following such letters may lead to imposition of more severe discipline.

Q.6:2 What is a summary suspension?

Summary suspension of privileges is drastic action that is taken without affording the affected staff member the opportunity for a prior hearing and, usually, without formal action by the hospital governing body. The hospital must be prepared to justify summary action on the basis of the need to protect the hospital's patients. Where no immediate danger to patients exists, summary revocation or suspension may not be upheld in court. [See, e.g., *McMillan v. Anchorage Community Hospital*, 646 P.2d 857 (Alaska 1982).]

In a situation involving a potential immediate risk to patient well-being, there is no requirement that a hearing be held prior to the imposition of restrictions on the practitioner. It is generally accepted, however, that a hearing must be granted the practitioner within a reasonable time following the summary suspension for the procedure to meet due process requirements. The HCQIA permits the immediate suspension or restriction of clinical privileges to avoid imminent danger to patients as long as due process procedures outlined in the law are subsequently afforded to the physician. [42 U.S.C. §11112(c) (1988)]

Q.6:3 Why does it matter who has the authority to summarily suspend?

Many bylaws authorize the CEO or a medical staff leader to implement a summary suspension. State peer review laws, however, generally protect only action taken by a committee, not action taken by an individual. There have been a few cases that have held that the state immunity provisions of the peer review law did not apply in a summary suspension situation because the action was taken by an individual. [See *Berry v. Oak Park Hosp.*, 628 N.E.2d 1159 (Ill. App. 1993).]

The HCQIA states that immunity applies to a summary suspension that is held consistent with the HCQIA and is based on a concern that failure to impose a suspension may result in imminent danger to the health of any individual.

Q.6:4 Must summary suspensions by reported to the NPDB?

A summary suspension is reportable if it is in effect for more than 30 days or it is imposed for a period longer than 30 days. It is based on the professional conduct of the practitioner that adversely affected or could adversely affect the health or welfare of a patient; it is the result of a professional review action taken by a hospital or other health care entity.

DHHS's *NPDB Guidebook Supplement* addresses the issue of summary suspensions but does not clarify the reportability issue. It may depend on how the bylaws are written. If the bylaws indicate that a summary suspension is not "a professional review action" until it is a final decision of the governing body after an opportunity for a hearing and an appeal, the summary suspension would not be reportable until it is affirmed by the governing body or until the appeal period has expired or the appeal procedures have been exhausted.

Q.6:5 Can inadequate clinical performance be used as grounds for termination?

The most common ground for termination, reduction or suspension of privileges, or other disciplinary action is inadequate or substandard clinical performance. [See, e.g., *Chouteau v. Enid Memorial Hospital*, 992 F.2d 1106 (10th Cir. 1993).] When the disciplinary action is taken on the basis of an adverse evaluation of the practitioner's professional competence, the courts will generally refrain from substituting their opinion for that of the medical staff and governing body. As long as the decision is a reasonable one, and not arbitrary and capricious, the courts will sustain it.

Q.6:6 Can inability to work with others be used as grounds for termination?

Inability to work with others may be another reason for disciplinary action. [See, e.g., *Landefeld v. Marion General Hospital*, 994 F.2d 1178 (6th Cir. 1993).] A medical staff member who is a disruptive force in the hospital may have his or her medical staff membership terminated or privileges reduced or suspended. According to one court, instances of ill temper, annoyance, or criticism of hospital policies or other physicians alone do not create a basis for revoking privileges. Instead, the hospital must show concrete evidence of specific instances of disruptive behavior. [*Nanavati v. Burdette Tomlin Memorial Hosp.*, 526 A.2d 697 (N.J. 1987)]

Q.6:7 Can infringement of hospital rules be grounds for discipline?

Imposition of lesser degrees of discipline on medical staff members for infringements of hospital rules unrelated to clinical practice is probably a relatively common event in most hospitals. Termination of staff membership or reduction of privileges because of a rule violation is undoubtedly less common, but this does not mean that hospitals may not take such drastic measures when rules are broken. Where a medical staff member repeatedly violated a hospital rule requiring the writing of a history and physical for the medical record, the court found that violation of the rule was a reasonable ground for dismissal of the practitioner from the staff. [*Anderson v. Board of Trustees of Caro Community Hosp.*, 159 N.W.2d 347 (Mich. App. 1968)]

Q.6:8 Can a low volume of admissions be used as a grounds for termination?

The medical staff bylaws may contain a minimum admissions requirement and specify that failure to meet that requirement is grounds for denial of reappointment. If the hospital uses this as a criterion, it must be able to show that it is based on quality of care issues to avoid fraud and abuse or antitrust allegations. A few courts have upheld failure to meet a minimum admissions requirement as a valid basis for reduction or termination of privileges. [*Saint Louis v. Baystate Medical Center, Inc.*, 568 N.E.2d 1181 (Mass. App. 1991)]

Q.6:9 Can failure to follow bylaws, rules and regulations, or policies be used as a grounds for discipline?

It is essential that all practitioners agree to follow the bylaws, rules and regulations, or policies of the facility. The hospital has a legal duty to carefully credential and monitor its medical staff. It can do so effectively only if it has the authority to enforce the requirements contained in its documents. Agreement to follow the bylaws, rules and regulations, or policies is generally included in the application for staff membership. Violation of this agreement has been held to be grounds for discipline. [See, e.g., *Friedman v. Delaware County Memorial Hospital*, 672 F. Supp. 171 (E.D. Pa. 1987), *aff'd*, 849 F.2d 600 (3d Cir. 1988).]

Q.6:10 Can unfavorable or unsatisfactory references be grounds for termination?

The hospital establishes requirements necessary for application and reapplication to the medical staff. Satisfactory references are one of the usual requirements. If a hospital receives unfavorable references, it has a duty to investigate further. It may determine on the basis of unfavorable references to reject the applicant. If decisions were not made on this basis, it would be superfluous to require references. [See, e.g., *Scott v. Sisters of St. Francis Health Services, Inc.*, 645 F. Supp. 1465 (N.D. Ill. 1986) *aff'd*, 822 F.2d 1090 (7th Cir. 1987).]

Q.6:11 What other grounds for termination have been upheld by courts?

Among the grounds for termination that have been upheld by courts are:

- **refusal to treat indigent patients** [*Rooney v. Medical Center Hospital*, (S.D. Ohio Mar. 30, 1994)]
- **restriction of privileges at other facilities** [*Rao v. Auburn General Hospital*, 573 P.2d 834 (Wash. App.), *review denied*, 90 Wash. 2d 1015 (1978)]
- **failure to purchase malpractice insurance** [*Stein v. Tri-City Hospital Authority*, 384 S.E.2d 430 (Ga. Ct. App, 1989), *cert. denied* (Ga. Sept. 29, 1989)]
- **failure to become board certified** [*Silverstein v. Gwinnett Hospital Authority*, 861 F.2d 1560 (11th Cir. 1988)]
- **substance abuse** [*Soentgen v. Quain & Ramstad Clinic*, 467 N.W.2d 73 (N.D. 1991)]
- **failure to meet training requirements** [*Flegel v. Christian Hospital*, 4 F.3d 682 (8th Cir. 1993)]
- **unfavorable report by proctor** [*Nicholson v. Lucas*, 26 Cal. Rptr. 2d 778 (Cal. App. 1994)]
- **criminal activity** [*Greenwald v. Department of Professional Regulation*, 501 So.2d 740 (Fla. App. 1987), *review denied*, 511 So.2d 998 (Fla.), *cert. denied*, 484 U.S. 986 (1987)]
- **loss of federal narcotics license** [*Paskon v. Salem Memorial Hospital District*, 806 S.W.2d 417 (Mo. App.), *cert. denied*, 112 S. Ct. 302 (1991)]

INVESTIGATION

Q.6:12 Who conducts an investigation into whether disciplinary action is necessary?

The fair hearing plan will specify how an investigation is to be initiated and who has the authority to do so. Usually, the CEO or the chief of staff has the authority to initiate an investigation. The investigation itself may be the responsibility of the medical executive committee or the credentials committee, which usually appoints an ad hoc committee to conduct the investigation.

In a large facility, the medical staff coordinator may be involved in gathering information for the investigation. If trained staff is not available, the hospital may hire special counsel to prepare for and conduct the hearing. The hospital's general counsel should not be involved at this point because he or she may need to advise the board when the peer review action reaches the appeals level.

Q.6:13 Must the practitioner be informed of the investigation?

Generally, a practitioner need not be informed of an investigation unless that is required by the bylaws. [See *Owens v. New Britain General Hospital*, 627 A.2d 1373 (Conn. App. Ct. 1993).] It may be that the committee investigating will find no grounds to proceed and the matter will be dropped with no formal action. As a practical matter, the physician may become aware of an investigation if the investigating committee needs documents or records in the physician's possession.

Q.6:14 What does the investigating committee do upon completion of its investigation?

The investigating committee informs the medical executive committee or the credentials committee in writing of the results of its investigation and submits its recommendations. The committee could recommend that no further action be taken due to insufficient evidence, or it could recommend various degrees of disciplinary action, some of which may trigger hearing rights, and some which may not.

Q.6:15 What action is taken after the investigating committee makes its recommendations?

The ad hoc committee makes its recommendations to the committee that appointed it. If that was the credentials committee, the credentials committee makes its recommendations to the medical executive committee, which makes its recommendations to the governing body.

Q.6:16 What happens if the investigative committee's recommendation will adversely affect the physician?

When the executive committee makes an adverse recommendation, the physician should receive notice of the adverse recommendation and the reasons for it. The practitioner should be informed of the right to request a hearing. If the practitioner does request a hearing in a timely manner, he or she should be given a detailed statement of the reasons for the adverse recommendation and should be given notice of the time and place of the hearing. The HCQIA also requires that the practitioner be given a list of witnesses.

Q.6:17 Is it appropriate to use an outside consultant to review a physician's medical records when clinical competence has been called into question?

There are situations in which the hospital may find that it is appropriate to use outside consultants. A provision for this option should be included in the bylaws or the fair hearing plan. A hospital may want to use an outside consultant if the medical staff of a hospital is small and the physicians who would be involved in peer review could be viewed as competitors. Use of an outside consultant will forestall charges of bias or conspiracy. Another reason to use an outside consultant may be that the medical staff physicians do not feel qualified to evaluate a particular physician. A third situation in which using an outside consultant might be appropriate is to review the clinical activity of a department that consists of one physician group. For example, a hospital may contract with a physician group to staff the emergency department. While it is possible for the physicians within the group to perform peer review, their close association and unity of interests may make peer review more awkward than usual. The hospital may decide that the use of an outside consultant would relieve this awkwardness and provide objective assurance that quality care is being rendered.

Q.6:18 At what point does an investigation become reportable?

Once a practitioner is "under investigation," any corrective action or settlement arising from the investigation may be reportable under state law or under the HCQIA. For this reason, many hospitals have opted to have a "preinvestigation" informal inquiry or interview that can clear up misunderstandings without triggering reporting requirements. This should be specified in the bylaws as an option.

HEARING

Q.6:19 Are all hospitals subject to due process requirements?

The Fifth Amendment to the U.S. Constitution prohibits the U.S. government from depriving any person of property without due process of law. The Fourteenth Amendment is held to apply this principle to the states and their subdivisions. Several states have constitutional provisions similar to those found in the federal constitution that are applicable within the state. Public hospitals, such as those operated by the state or county, are required to preserve the constitutional rights of practitioners to both substantive and procedural due process regarding medical staff appointment and privileges.

There is a large body of law addressing the question of whether due process requirements apply to private hospitals. The answer turns on whether the hospital is viewed as engaging in state action, which would render it subject to due process requirements. As one court stated, "In the absence of a showing, allegation or admission that the Hospital's action reflected state action . . ., fundamental constitutional due process may not be invoked." [*Garrow v. Elizabeth Gen. Hosp. and Dispensary*, 401 A.2d 533 , at 563 (N.J. 1979)] The court went on to state, however, that while aggrieved physicians have no right to constitutional due process, they are entitled to "fundamental fairness," which means that their request for privileges be considered according to procedures that adequately notify them of the hospital's proposed action and provide a reasonable opportunity to respond.

Some courts have found that private hospitals are engaged in state action and are public in character because they accept government funds, provide services to the public, and, in the case of nonprofit institutions, are tax-exempt. Many courts, however, are reluctant to attribute state action to private hospitals in spite of governmental entanglement in the daily operations of most private hospitals.

While private hospitals may or may not be constitutionally required to do so, the reality is that they generally do provide a fairly high level of due process. This is especially true of hospitals that seek the benefit of the HCQIA's immunity provisions and, therefore, follow the procedural rules set out in that law.

Q.6:20 What is due process?

There are two aspects to due process: substantive and procedural. Substantive due process refers to rights that must be protected. For example, if state law mandates that medical staffs comprise allopathic physicians, osteopathic physicians, dentists, and podiatrists, each type of practitioner listed has been given the substantive right to be considered for medical staff membership and cannot be categorically denied because of their school of practice. If they are discriminated against on that basis, that is a violation of substantive due process. That does not mean that every physician, dentist, and podiatrist has a right to be granted medical staff membership or privileges. Each applicant must meet all of the admission criteria and must be individually evaluated and approved.

The mainstay of substantive due process is reasonableness. Hospitals that are subject to due process limitations must make rules for governing the medical staff that are reasonably calculated to achieve some legitimate hospital purpose. They must not be arbitrary or capricious or vague. Hospital bylaws and rules dealing with the qualifications for medical staff membership and privileges or limiting professional discretion within the hospital are examples of measures that must be reasonable and clear in order to comport with substantive due process.

Procedural due process refers to the procedures put in place to protect the substantive rights. It can be thought of as fundamental fairness. There are several elements that have come to be accepted as necessary to establish procedural due process. A right to notice, to be informed of the facts relied on as the basis for an adverse action as well as what hospital rule or bylaw is being applied, is essential. There is also the right to be heard, to present evidence and argument in opposition to the adverse action, and to confront those whose testimony provided the facts being relied on by the body taking action. The practitioner must be given a reasonable amount of time to prepare for the hearing and reasonable access to records in the possession of the hospital that were used as the basis of the adverse action. A fair hearing includes the right to be heard by an unbiased tribunal. The practitioner is entitled to a written determination of the outcome, which must be forthcoming within a reasonable amount of time. The practitioner should also be given the opportunity to appeal the decision within a reasonable amount of time. The HCQIA includes specific time limits.

Q.6:21 Does every action against staff membership or privileges require due process protections?

Due process protections need not be extended to practitioners whose privileges have been adversely affected for reasons unrelated to competence. The courts have upheld this principle.

- *Englestad v. Virginia Municipal Hosp.*, 718 F.2d 262 (8th Cir. 1983).—A physician who had an oral, terminable-at-will contract to provide pathology services for a municipal hospital had no constitutionally protected property interest in continued employment and could not invoke procedural due process rights upon his termination.
- *Dutta v. St. Francis Regional Med. Center*, 867 P.2d 1057 (Kan. 1994).—A radiologist was not entitled to a hearing upon revocation of her access to radiology facilities when a hospital entered into an exclusive contract with another radiologist because the hospital was making a managerial decision based on business considerations.
- *Abrams v. St. John's Hospital*, 30 Cal. Rptr.2d 603 (App. Ct. 1994).—Physicians who obtain exclusive contracts to supply medical services to hospitals are bound by contractual termination provisions waiving due process hearing rights.

Q.6:22 What due process rights are health care entities legally required to provide?

That depends on state law to a large extent. State statutes and regulations may require that certain due process procedures be afforded to practitioners. In addition, there may be court decisions that govern whether certain procedures are required in a particular jurisdiction.

Q.6:23 How does the HCQIA fit in with due process requirements?

The Health Care Quality Improvement Act (HCQIA) is a federal law that provides immunity to peer reviewers who follow certain due process procedures set out in the law. Health care entities are not required to abide by the HCQIA due process provisions. In addition, HCQIA immunity applies only to "professional review actions," defined as actions or recommendations "based on the competence or professional conduct of an individual physician which conduct affects or could affect adversely the health or welfare of a patient or patients . . . ." Therefore, a health care entity may elect to follow the HCQIA due process requirements only when an adverse action is based on the competence or professional conduct of a practitioner so that the immunity provisions will apply.

Q.6:24 What procedural requirements are necessary to trigger the immunity provisions of the HCQIA?

The immunity provisions of the HCQIA apply only if the challenged peer review action was taken in the reasonable belief that the action was in the furtherance of quality health care, the action was taken after reasonable effort to obtain the facts of the matter, the entity afforded the affected physician adequate notice and hearing procedures, and there was a reasonable belief that the action was warranted. [42 U.S.C. §§1101-11152]

To provide adequate notice to a physician, a hospital must substantially comply with the notice requirements outlined in the statute, as follows:

- The physician under review must be notified that a professional review action against him or her has been proposed.
- The physician must be given the reasons for the proposed action.
- The physician must have the opportunity to request a hearing by a specified date, which must be at least 30 days after the notice.
- The physician must be notified of the rights the physician will have at the hearing.
- If the physician requests a hearing, the physician must receive another notice that identifies the place, time, and date of the hearing, which cannot be held earlier than 30 days after the second notice. The second notice must also identify the witnesses who will testify on behalf of the professional review body at the hearing.

Hospitals seeking to invoke HCQIA immunity must also substantially comply with the following hearing requirements:

- The hearing must be before a mutually acceptable arbitrator, hearing officer, or panel of individuals who are not direct competitors of the physician.
- The physician can be represented by a person of his or her choice, including an attorney.
- The physician has the right to examine and cross-examine witnesses.
- The physician has the right to present whatever other evidence he or she wishes, including testimony.
- The physician also has the right to provide a written statement at the hearing's conclusion.
- The physician has a right to have a copy of the hearing transcript at the physician's cost. The professional review body's decision must be in writing, include the basis on which the decision was made, and be transmitted to the physician.
- The health care entity also must provide the physician with a written decision incorporating the basis of its decision.

Q.6:25 What if the due process procedures described in the HCQIA are not fully adhered to?

The HCQIA states that failure to provide all of the listed procedural rights does not lead to the conclusion that the proceeding was unfair. Health care entities can prove that even though their procedures differed from those specified in the HCQIA, they were nonetheless sufficient. The law does not mandate specific hearing procedures but states that if certain procedural rights are afforded, a presumption of fairness arises that will trigger the granting of immunities created by the law. The HCQIA permits the physician to rebut this presumption of fairness. Because the law sets forth the procedures that will ensure immunity, most health care entities striving to attain such immunity make sure their procedures mirror those listed in the HCQIA.

Q.6:26 What was the first case to apply the immunities available under the HCQIA?

The first case to apply the immunities of HCQIA was Austin v. McNamara, in which the Ninth Circuit ruled that a physician peer review committee had met all the due process requirements under HCQIA and was, therefore, shielded from antitrust liability. A neurosurgeon had been summarily suspended due to concerns about the quality of the medical treatment he had been rendering. He was granted a hearing regarding the suspension, as provided in the medical staff bylaws. A judicial review committee subsequently decided that the summary suspension was unreasonable and recommended the physician's reinstatement to the staff but, due to evidence of substandard care, required that he be subject to internal consultations and outside neurosurgical review. The physician sued in federal court alleging antitrust violations, but the trial court dismissed the suit based on the HCQIA. [731 F. Supp. 934 (C.D. Cal. 1990), *aff'd*, 979 F.2d (9th Cir. 1992)]

The Ninth Circuit agreed that the hospital and peer reviewers were protected from antitrust liability because all HCQIA requirements had been met. To invoke the protections of the law, there must be reasonable belief that the action would further the quality of health care, reasonable effort to obtain the facts, adequate notice and hearing, and reasonable belief that the facts warranted the action. If these standards are met there is a presumption of fairness that can be rebutted only by a preponderance of the evidence. The court ruled that the standards had been met and that the judicial review committee's reinstatement of the physician did not rebut the reasonableness of the peer reviewers' action. It found that due to the severe restrictions the judicial review committee imposed on the physician, a reasonable jury could not find that the peer review committee's actions were unreasonable. Finally, the court ruled that the HCQIA applied to the case although much of the peer review activity occurred before the law was enacted because the entire peer review process was not completed until after the effective date of the law.

Q.6:27 If a hospital follows the requirements of the HCQIA, does it automatically meet the requirements of state law?

Following the requirements of the HCQIA does not ensure compliance with state law. State law may impose additional or stricter requirements that hospitals must meet. In one case, for example, an anesthesiologist sued a hospital because it allowed nonmedical personnel to be members of a peer review committee. The state peer review statute requires that peer review committees be composed entirely of medical staff members. The hospital contended, however, that it was following the HCQIA, which does not require that peer review committee members be medical staff members. The court granted a permanent injunction forbidding nonmedical staff members from being members of the peer review committee. It held that the HCQIA does not limit a state's right to impose additional safeguards. [*Mann v. Johnson Hospital*, 611 N.E.2d 676 (Ind. Ct. App. 1993)]

Q.6:28 If the procedural requirements of the HCQIA have been followed, thereby triggering the immunity provisions, does that mean that a hospital cannot be sued?

While earlier cases indicated that hospitals that followed the procedural requirements of the HCQIA could not be sued, more recent cases have made a distinction between being sued and being liable for damages. The courts are now indicating that the act does not grant the right to be free from trial and are allowing physicians to sue despite the immunities available to peer reviewers under the HCQIA. [See *Manion v. Evans*, 986 F.2d 1036 (6th Cir. 1993).]

Q.6:29 When does a physician have a right to a hearing?

The bylaws should specify when a right to a hearing arises. If a physician's clinical competence or professional behavior is called into question and the matter is dealt with informally, such as through peer counseling, but the physician's privileges are not implicated, there is no right to a hearing. If, on the other hand, a physician's clinical competence or professional behavior is called into question and there is action taken against that practitioner's membership or privileges, this will trigger a right to a hearing.

- Some state laws indicate that practitioners have a right to a hearing when an application is denied.
- The Joint Commission requires a fair hearing and appeal process for addressing adverse decisions for the applicant regarding medical staff appointment or reappointment and granting of initial or renewed/revised clinical privileges. [MS 2.12.1 (1994)]
- The bylaws may state that there is no right to a hearing if the physician's privileges are suspended due to failure to complete medical records. This is more of an administrative matter that can be resolved upon completion of the delinquent records and does not involve a question of competence.
- An investigation into whether particular conduct warrants disciplinary action does not of itself give rise to a right to a hearing. The investigation may reveal that such action is unnecessary.
- In an exclusive contract scenario, the contract itself may specify that if the contract is terminated for reasons other than clinical competence, there will be no right to a hearing. The contract should also provide that if an exclusive contract is terminated, the clinical privileges of the physicians in the group will automatically be terminated as well. Conversely, if clinical privileges of the physicians are terminated, the contract will also be terminated.

Q.6:30 What if the physician does not request a hearing within the specified time?

The HCQIA states that practitioners should have 30 days from notice of the proposed adverse action to request a hearing. The hospital's fair hearing plan should indicate that failure to request a hearing within the specified time period results in a waiver of the right to a hearing.

Q.6:31 Are the procedural rules of the hearing the same as those used in a trial?

The hearing procedures need not be as extensive as those used in a trial. The fair hearing plan should indicate the scope of the procedures that will be used during the hearing. Formal discovery, for example, which includes the taking of depositions and the right to compel production of documents, generally is not part of the hearing process. At the very least, the practitioner should be given access to the medical records used as the basis of the adverse hearing and other documentation relied on or to be presented to the committee or hearing officer.

Discovery is generally not as extensive or as formal. The HCQIA does not require discovery. State law, however, may impose various requirements. In California, for example, practitioners have the right to inspect and copy documentary evidence that is relevant to the charges as long as the documents do not refer solely to another practitioner. [Cal. Bus. & Prof. Code §809.2(d)]

Q.6:32 Who is on the hearing panel?

The panel will comprise other medical staff members and a hearing officer.

The physicians serving on the hearing panel must not be the individuals involved in the investigation or initial decision to impose the adverse action. In addition, panel members should not have a history of antagonism, bias, or prejudice against the practitioner. Finally, the hearing panel members should not be in direct economic competition with the practitioner.

As an alternative to a hearing panel comprised of medical staff members, the HCQIA allows a hearing before a single hearing officer who is not in economic competition with the affected practitioner. It also permits a hearing by an arbitrator who is agreeable to both the facility and the practitioner. [*Hackenthal v. California Medical Association*, 138 Cal. App. 3d 435 (1982)] (Investigators should not serve on hearing panel.) [*Applebaum v. Board of Directors of Barton Memorial Hospital*, 104 Cal. App. 3d 648 (1980)] (Hearing panel members should be free of bias.)

Q.6:33 What is the role of the hearing officer?

The hearing officer establishes the procedural ground rules, makes judgments regarding such procedures, such as the admissibility of specific evidence, and generally controls the flow of the hearing. The hearing officer is often independent local counsel.

Q.6:34 What is the role of hospital counsel in the hearing process?

Hospital counsel should not be involved in the hearing process because counsel may be called upon to advise the governing body on appeal. Earlier involvement may supply grounds for charges of bias.

Q.6:35 Can a physician submit evidence in his or her defense that other physicians are guilty of the same conduct as a defense?

There are several cases that hold such evidence is irrelevant and is not admissible. [See, e.g., *Smith v. Ricks*, 798 F. Supp. 605 (N.D. Cal. 1992), which relied on HCQIA.]

Q.6:36 Is hearsay evidence admissible in a hearing?

Hearsay evidence that has rational probative force and that is corroborated may be used as evidence in a disciplinary hearing. [See, e.g., *Mahmoodian v. United Hospital Center*, 404 S.E.2d 750

(W.Va.), *cert. denied*, 112 S. Ct. 185 (1991).] Because evidentiary rules are not as strict as those used at trial, the hearing officer is more likely to admit evidence, as long as the process is not being abused. Doing so provides less grounds for challenge should the matter end up in court.

Q.6:37 When a physician is challenging a hearing panel on grounds of bias, must the physician prove actual bias, or is potential bias sufficient?

Case law indicates that a physician must prove actual bias in such situations. [See, e.g., *Richards v. Emanuel County Hospital Authority*, 603 F. Supp. 81 (S.D. Ga. 1984).]

Q.6:38 Is it permissible to admit new charges or additional evidence against a practitioner that was not indicated in the charges before the hearing?

New charges or additional evidence may be admitted, but only after the practitioner is given notice and reasonable time to prepare a response to the new charges or to examine the additional evidence. This is necessary to ensure compliance with due process. This possibility should be addressed in the bylaws. [See, e.g., *Fobbs v. Holy Cross Health System Corporation*, 789 F. Supp. 1054 (E.D. Cal. 1992).]

In addition to case law, the legislative history of the HCQIA supports this position as well, as indicated by the following excerpt:

> The Committee is aware that between the time the initial notice is given of a proposed professional review action and the time of the hearing on that action, the investigation may have uncovered reasons for such an action other than or in addition to the reasons specified in the initial notice. Provided that notice is given in a way that protects the interests of the physicians against whom the action is proposed, a supplemental notice of such additional reasons might well satisfy the requirements of due process. [H.R. Rep. No. 903, 99th Cong., 2d Sess. 10]

Q.6:39 What happens if procedural issues are discussed at the outset of a hearing, but the practitioner does not raise any objections until later?

If the practitioner does not raise objections at the beginning of the hearing, the right to do so may be waived. [See, e.g., *Kennedy v. St. Joseph Memorial Hospital of Kokomo, Indiana Inc.*, 482 N.E.2d 268 (Ind. App. 1985), *aff'd*, 536 N.E.2d 274 (1989).]

Q.6:40 Should the proceedings be recorded?

Although the services of a transcriber are expensive, having an accurate record of the hearing may be essential for proving to a court that due process was accorded. The HCQIA indicates the right to have the hearing recorded but does not specify who must pay for it. The facility and practitioner may agree to share the costs.

Q.6:41 To what material must the practitioner be given access?

The main consideration is fairness. The practitioner should have an opportunity to explain and defend against the information used as the basis of the adverse recommendation. The practitioner should have access to copies of the medical records, incident reports, or other documents on which the adverse recommendation was made. The right to discovery will vary with state law. California, for example, mandates the discovery of "documentary information relevant to the charges" that either party has in its possession and control. [Cal. Bus. and Prof. Code, §809.2(d)] Other states may have other requirements or may have addressed the issue in case law.

Q.6:42 Is there a requirement that the practitioner notify the medical staff of the witnesses expected to testify on his or her behalf?

If a hospital is following the mandates of the HCQIA, the prehearing notice must contain a list of witnesses expected to testify at the hearing on behalf of the medical staff.

There is no requirement, however, that the practitioner notify the medical staff of the witnesses expected to testify on his or her behalf. State law may impose such a requirement, however, such as the law in California. [Cal. Bus. & Prof. Code, §809.2(f)] In addition, this requirement may be imposed by including it in the bylaws.

Q.6:43 Can the practitioner question the members of the hearing panel to ensure lack of bias?

Voir dire is a process by which the practitioner questions the prospective members of the panel to try to determine whether they are biased. Whether the practitioner is entitled to question prospective panel members depends on the case law and statutory law of the jurisdiction as well as on the parameters established in the fair hearing plan. At least one court has ruled that such questioning cannot be unfairly limited. [*Lasko v. Valley Presbyterian Hospital.* 180 Cal App. 3d 435 (1982)] California law permits *voir dire* of potential panel members and the hearing officer. [Cal. Bus. & Prof. Code §809.2(a),(c)]

Q.6:44 Does the practitioner have the right to be represented by an attorney at the hearing?

Whether there is a right to legal counsel in an *advocacy* role during hearing proceedings may depend on state law. The courts have ruled both ways on this issue. The HCQIA hearing requirements specify that the practitioner is entitled to representation by any person of his or her choice, including an attorney. The law does not specify, however, what the scope of that role is or how much the hospital can limit the attorney's role.

Q.6:45 Who has the burden of proof when there has been an adverse recommendation of the medical staff?

The bylaws should put the burden on the aggrieved practitioner to establish by clear and convincing proof that the hospital's decision was unreasonable. The courts have upheld this requirement. [See *Rosenblit v. Superior Court of Orange County*, 282 Cal. Rptr. 819 (Cal. App. 1991), *review denied*, (Sept. 19, 1991).]

Q.6:46 What questions should a health care facility ask to determine whether the hearing was fair?

The following questionnaire was developed by a health care attorney as an aid to determine whether the peer review process has been perverted to accomplish malicious ends. That situation is rare. However, the questionnaire does provide a good review of elements to focus on to ensure a fair peer review process.

Malice Barometer

As to the complaining physician or other person requesting the peer review (if any):

1. Is there any evidence or allegation that the complainant has personal ill will, hatred, or contempt for the accused physician?
2. Has the complainant initiated any litigation against the accused physician and, if so, is it possible that the complainant could improve his position in the litigation by instituting the complaint?
3. Has the complainant sought any other forum to complain about the same accused physician, such as medical societies, professional associations, or other medical staff proceedings?
4. Is there a credible challenge to the reliability, integrity, or honesty of the complainant?

As to the reviewing physicians:

5. Did the reviewing physicians spend approximately the same period of time (if any) with the complainant and the accused?
6. Were the reviewing physicians chosen on a system or basis according to established and fair criteria, to prevent the complainant or the accused physician from having any role in their selection?

---

7. Does the complainant or accused physician have any significant social or professional association with the reviewing physicians that might bias their opinion?
8. Is there any other reason why the reviewing physicians might be biased in favor of the complainant and against the accused physician?

As to the written peer review report:

9. Did the reviewers adequately investigate the facts, including a review of any pertinent medical records?
10. Did they adequately check any sources other than medical records for relevant materials not contained in the record?
11. Did they prepare and sign an accurate and thorough written report?
12. If the process allows for such an opportunity, did the reviewers talk to the accused physician before publication of the final report and did they fairly reflect or acknowledge the accused physician's perspective?
13. If errors in the written report were pointed out prior to or after publication, and the reviewers were specifically put on notice, did they adequately follow up and check their facts?
14. Does the written report materially distort and exaggerate certain facts so that a reader could be misled?
15. Does the peer review report contain false statements?
16. Does the written report conceal facts favorable to the accused physician or disregard substantial evidence favorable to the accused physician?
17. Does the written report present a fair, objective, and balanced analysis of the care received by the patient or other behavior in question and does it avoid an inappropriate focus on unimportant, minor problems?

18. If the accused physician retained his or her own consultant to prepare a report, and if the reviewers received a copy of the report, did they carefully read it, consider its contents, and acknowledge the report in a fair manner?
19. If the accused physician's consultant assumed different facts, did the reviewers follow up and investigate further?
20. In situations where a number of cases are being reviewed, does the written report carefully analyze the "good" cases as well as the "bad" in order to show balance and objectivity?

[Baker, C.H., "A Proposal for a Malice Barometer in Physician Peer Review: Twenty Questions You Should Ask," *Issues in Hospital Law: Selected Key Articles from Hospital Law Newsletter*, ed. N. Hershey, (Gaithersburg, MD: Aspen Publishers, Inc., 1989), 39–40]

Q.6:47 What happens at the conclusion of the hearing?

The fair hearing plan may permit or require both sides to submit a written summary of their positions. The hearing panel should prepare a written decision stating the basis for its conclusions. [Required by the HCQIA 42 U.S.C. §11112 (b)(3)(D)(ii)] This establishes a clear record of the basis of the decision in the event the hearing is reviewed by a court.

The practitioner must be notified of the hearing board's recommendation and informed of the right to request appellate review. The HCQIA requires that a practitioner must be given an opportunity to appeal an adverse hearing panel report before the hospital governing board makes its final decision.

The hearing panel forwards its decision to the governing body, which is the final authority for imposing disciplinary measures.

Q.6:48 Can the board impose a stricter penalty than the one recommended?

In *Siqueira v. Northwestern Memorial Hospital*, 477 N.E.2d 16 (Ill. App. 1985), the court ruled that a physician in this situation was not entitled to an extra hearing.

Q.6:49 What is the proper scope of an appeal?

The governing body conducts an appeal of an adverse decision in accordance with the procedures specified in the fair hearing plan or the bylaws. The appeal may be heard by the entire governing body or by a subcommittee. The appeal should be limited to the issues of whether the hearing was conducted properly and fairly and whether the evidence supports the final recommendation.

Q.6:50 If the HCQIA hearing requirements are violated, can a practitioner sue on that basis?

Due process rights contained in the HCQIA are not mandatory. The HCQIA is not an affirmative law that imposes requirements. It is up to the facility to determine if it wants to gain the immunity available by following the procedures specified in the law.

At least one federal appeals court has ruled that a physician may not sue a health care entity for failing to comply with HCQIA hearing requirements. [*Hancock v. Blue Cross–Blue Shield of Kansas*, No. 93-3054 (10th Cir. April 11, 1994)] In that case, a physician claimed that an insurer violated his right to counsel under the HCQIA because his attorney could not cross-examine witnesses or present an argument at a decredentialing hearing. The court held that the HCQIA does not create a private cause of action and dismissed the suit.

LEGAL CHALLENGES

Q.6:51 What are the most common types of judicial relief sought by a practitioner whose medical staff privileges or membership has been restricted or revoked?

One of the first impulses of a practitioner whose medical staff privileges or membership has been restricted or revoked is to seek legal redress by filing a lawsuit. Judicial remedies may not be immediately available to the practitioner, however, and a number of limitations may exist that render judicial action not wholly satisfactory to him or her. The most common forms of relief sought are:

- mandatory injunctions requiring the hospital to appoint or reinstate the practitioner
- injunctions prohibiting the hospital from excluding the practitioner
- declaratory judgments holding the practitioner entitled to hospital membership and privileges
- monetary damages for injury to reputation or interference with the practitioner's professional income or contractual relationships

Q.6:52 Can a practitioner immediately take his or her grievance to the courts?

If the hospital has a mechanism that provides for a hearing on the merits of the affected practitioner's loss of membership or privileges that requires internal procedures to be exhausted and provides that the result of the internal procedure is "final," the courts will normally require that the internal remedies available to the practitioner be exhausted before an action may be brought in court. [See, e.g., *Yarnell v. Sisters of St. Francis Health Servs.*, 446 N.E.2d 359 (Ind. Ct. App. 1983).] If the practitioner refuses to participate in the hearing, fails to appear, or leaves the hearing while it is in progress, the courts probably will not entertain a contention that procedural due process rights were denied. However, if the procedure that is afforded by the hospital is patently devoid of fundamental due process guarantees, the affected practitioner may be justified in refusing to participate. [See *Garrow v. Elizabeth Gen. Hosp. & Dispensary*, 382 A.2d 393 (N.J. Super. Ct. 1977) *modified*, 401 A.2d 533 (N.J. 1979).] It is reasonable to expect that the exhaustion of administrative remedies will be a prerequisite to judicial review in all but a very small minority of cases.

Q.6:53 Are practitioners always entitled to judicial review?

Some states have ruled that judicial review is prohibited even if administrative remedies have been exhausted. A New Jersey appeals court declared that a physician could not relitigate a private hospital's decision to terminate the physician's medical staff privileges if that decision was made in good faith after a fundamentally fair proceeding and was based on sufficiently reliable evidence. [*Zoneraich v. Overlook Hosp.*, 514 A.2d 53 (N.J. Super. Ct. App. Div. 1986)] Illinois, Florida, and Indiana courts have also ruled that judicial review of a private hospital's medical staff decisions is prohibited. Going one step further, a Michigan appeals court ruled that the bar on judicial review applied even if the private hospital acted arbitrarily, capriciously, or unreasonably. [*Sarin v. Samaritan Health Center*, 440 N.W.2d 80 (1989)]

There are some jurisdictions, however, that have ruled the other way. The Connecticut Supreme Court, for example, has ruled that decisions affecting a physician's medical staff privileges at a private nonprofit hospital are subject to judicial review. [*Gianetti v. Norwalk Hosp.*, 557 A.2d 1249 (Conn. 1989)] The court ruled that because contract issues are subject to judicial review and medical staff bylaws are part of a contractual relationship between the physician and the hospital, actions taken under the bylaws are subject to judicial review.

Q.6:54 On what grounds can a health care facility attempt to block the reinstatement of a practitioner while legal proceedings are pending?

To obtain a temporary injunction requiring reinstatement, a physician must show that if he or she is not reinstated, the physician will suffer irreparable harm, that there is no adequate legal relief (monetary damages), and that there is a likelihood of success on the merits of contention that the physician's privileges were wrongfully terminated.

- A showing of irreparable harm is an essential prerequisite to the issuance of a temporary injunction in most, if not all, jurisdictions. It may be difficult to obtain immediate reinstatement to full privileges on the medical staff through a temporary injunction pending final judicial determination of the case if the practitioner cannot demonstrate that he or she will suffer immediate harm that cannot be compensated for by money unless he or she is given staff privileges at once. [See *Kreuetzer v. Clark*, 607 S.W.2d 670 (Ark. 1980).] Allegations that the practitioner's patients may be deprived of hospital care as a basis for irreparable harm may fail if the institution can demonstrate that other hospitals are available or that another provider can care for the affected practitioner's patients. It may also be very difficult for the practitioner to show the likelihood of success on the merits of the case.

- A requirement that the practitioner post bond is common to all jurisdictions as a condition of issuing a temporary injunction. Immediate relief by use of a temporary injunction may be forestalled because of the difficulty in setting the amount of bond. Since the bond requirement is for the purpose of protecting the hospital from possible loss during the pendency of the temporary injunction, if serious clinical deficiencies were the cause of the termination of privileges, the hospital might argue convincingly that the bond should be adequate protection from any malpractice judgment rendered against it as a result of the practitioner's being permitted to exercise hospital privileges under a temporary injunction. A bond to cover such a contingency would make it difficult to find a surety and could be in excess of several million dollars. The premium for such a bond could be prohibitive.

- Framing an injunctive order reinstating a practitioner to the medical staff may be very difficult for the court. Staff privileges are granted as a result of hospital committee and department action and entail considerable discretionary evaluation by the medical profession. In order to accomplish its purpose, the injunction would have to direct each medical staff member and governing body member having responsibility for granting privileges to exercise individual discretion and not to exclude the practitioner or limit his or her privileges. Such an order would be arduous to draft and would compel the court to assume the responsibility of the medical staff and governing body for the hospital's operation and for the practitioner's performance and to render medical evaluations that a court is not equipped to do.

- Events occurring subsequent to an injunction granting a practitioner medical staff privileges may result in the medical staff and governing body once again terminating or suspending the practitioner, this time for reasons other than those used originally to exclude the practitioner. The court may deal with this problem by simply prohibiting the hospital from taking any action against the practitioner, but that would require the court to assume sole responsibility for the professional performance of the practitioner, an event that is not likely to occur. In addition, regardless of the existence of an order permitting the practitioner the use of the hospital, other members of the medical staff may refuse to work with the affected practitioner and deny him or her referrals, consultations, and the like, and, thereby, effectively limit or prohibit his or her practice in the institution. There is always the concern that such refusals may themselves give rise to an assertion that a conspiracy has been established by those members of the medical staff.

CONFIDENTIALITY ISSUES—DISCOVERABILITY AND ADMISSIBILITY

Q.6:55 What is the difference between discoverability and admissibility?

Discoverability involves access to documents or witnesses. Admissibility concerns whether documents, objects, or testimony may be admitted into evidence at trial. Information may be discoverable but not admissible. The law varies by state, and the federal courts have their own rules regarding discovery and admissibility that override state law.

Q.6:56 What are subpoenas and court orders?

Hospitals customarily receive two types of subpoenas: (1) a written order commanding a person to appear and give testimony at a trial or other judicial or investigative proceeding, and (2) a written order commanding a person to appear, give testimony, and bring all documents, papers, books, or records described in the subpoena. Subpoenas are used to obtain documents during pretrial discovery and to obtain testimony during trial.

A state or federal court or state commission may order a hospital to release medical records or other confidential patient information or to produce patient records in court. Written court orders are usually served upon hospitals in a manner similar to that of subpoenas, but court orders may also be issued verbally in court to a hospital's attorney.

Q.6:57 Do the states have laws regarding whether peer review records are discoverable?

States have peer review statutes that vary widely. (See Appendix A for a state-by-state breakdown of peer review statutes and case law.) Some laws provide that committee records generally are not subject to subpoena, discovery, or disclosure; others state that such records are not discoverable or describe such material as confidential or privileged. Many statutes contain an exception permitting physicians to discover records of staff privilege committees when contesting the termination, suspension, or limitation of their staff privileges. Most nondiscovery statutes state that the laws are not to be interpreted as protecting from discovery information, documents, and records that are otherwise available from original sources.

Q.6:58 What are some examples of peer review documents that might be shielded from discovery?

There are numerous types of documents that can be considered peer review documents; some are protectable, some are not. These documents should be treated as confidential documents. Language should be picked up directly from the state statute and incorporated into peer review documents in an effort to bring them within the protection of the law as confidential peer review documents. Examples of both confidential and nonconfidential peer review documents include:

- patient complaints
- privilege delineation forms
- profiling data
- audits
- outcome reports
- screening criteria
- medical records
- incident reports
- material from outside sources
- Data Bank inquiries
- preapplication materials
- application materials
- reappointment materials
- research studies
- credentialing data
- UR/QA reports
- committee minutes and policies
- release forms
- corporate bylaws
- medical staff bylaws
- rules and regulations
- department policies
- fair hearing plan

Q.6:59 Are application forms and reappointment forms discoverable?

Whether application forms and reappointment forms are considered confidential peer review documents protected from discovery depends on state law. In Illinois, for example, case law holds that information in appointment forms is not peer review material and is not protected.

In a California case, on the other hand, the state supreme court overturned an appeals court's order compelling a hospital to disclose physicians' applications and reapplications for staff privileges to a person suing for malpractice, ruling that state law protects this material from discovery. [*Alexander v. Superior Court of Los Angeles County*, B062903 (Cal. Oct. 14, 1993)]

In another variation, South Carolina's highest court held that a physician's application for staff privileges and supporting documentation are protected from discovery, but the outcome of the credentialing committee's deliberations is not. The supreme court agreed with the lower court that information that is available from another source does not become privileged simply by being acquired by the review committee. However, the court ruled, individuals seeking discovery cannot obtain documents that are available from original sources directly from the hospital committee but must seek them from alternative sources. The court also ruled that the state confidentiality law does not bar discovery of the general policies and procedures for staff monitoring. [*McGee v. Bruce Hospital System*, No. 23968 (S.C. Dec. 13, 1993)]

Whether such information is discoverable may also depend on what kind of suit is filed. For example, a federal trial court in Pennsylvania ruled that medical staff privileges files were discoverable in a federal antitrust case. A radiation therapy cancer center claimed that its business had failed due to a concerted effort by certain physicians and hospitals to drive it out of business. Part of this effort, the center alleged, included one hospital's delay in granting staff privileges to the director of the center. It, therefore, sought to discover documents from the hospital's staff privileges files. The hospital, however, contended that the center had a sufficient sample of the staff privileges files to allow it to ascertain that the director was granted privileges in a timely manner and that further discovery was irrelevant. It also argued that the files were protected from discovery by state and federal peer review statutes. [*Swarthmore Radiation Oncology Inc. v. Lapes*, No. 92-3055 (E.D. Pa. Nov. 15, 1993)]

The court granted the center's request for further discovery of the medical staff privileges files. It held that while the director's treatment was not central to the conspiracy theory, it is a subplot that could contribute to the ultimate success of the boycott claim. To prove discrimination, the court reasoned, there must be a comparison of how the hospital treated similarly situated physicians. The court rejected the contention that the staff privileges files are protected by state and federal peer review statutes. While the HCQIA requires reported medical staff information to be kept confidential, if the staff privileges application process is tainted by anticompetitive motives, it is not protected under the act, the court explained. In this case, the hospital, therefore, cannot claim a federal statutory peer review privilege, the court ruled. In addition, the court held that although the state peer review statute would shield the files from discovery, multiple federal interests override the state's interests. Federal rules embody a liberal policy of discovery, the court explained.

If there is no clear answer (and even if there is), the best way to deal with these forms is to treat them as confidential documents. The forms themselves should state that they are confidential, and they should be treated that way by all hospital and medical staff personnel.

Q.6:60 Does case law address whether peer review committee records are discoverable?

There is a substantial body of case law, which varies from state to state, that addresses whether peer review committee records are discoverable. Although state statutes have been enacted that address the issue of discoverability, some courts have interpreted such statutes broadly, while other courts interpret them narrowly. The following cases present a sampling of these approaches:

- *Posey v. District Court*, 586 P.2d 36 (Colo. 1978).

  Colorado statute that prohibited the subpoena of review committee records "in any suit against the physician" barred the subpoena of records in any civil suit, including one against a hospital.

- *Hollowell v. Jove*, 279 S.E.2d 430 (Ga. 1981).

  Georgia statute that prohibited the discovery of the "proceedings and records" of review committees included the records of a medical review committee relating to the care of patients other than the person suing.

- *Cedars-Sinai Medical Center v. Superior Court*, No. B066187 (Cal. Ct. App. 1993).

  Under the California peer review statute, the identities of hospital medical staff review committee members cannot be discovered in a medical malpractice case.

- *Matchett v. Superior Court for County of Yuba*, 115 Cal. Rptr. 317 (Ct. App. 1974).

  While credentials committee records may be privileged, hospital administration records were not covered by the state's nondiscovery law.

- *Marchand v. Henry Ford Hospital*, 247 N.W.2d 280 (Mich.1976).

  A law that protects information "collected for or by individuals or committees assigned [a quality] review function" does not protect data obtained by physicians on their initiative and later presented to a review committee.

Federal rules of evidence favor liberal discovery. In federal cases, state statutory privileges may not apply. A federal court in California, for example, ruled that a physician suing a hospital for federal antitrust damages after it had terminated his staff privileges could discover the records of the peer review that led to his termination. [*Pagano v. Oroville Hospital*, 145 F.R.D. 683 (E.D. Cal. 1993)] Similarly, the Seventh Circuit permitted discovery in a federal antitrust case brought by a physician who alleged restraint of trade by a group of competing physicians who allegedly had misused a hospital's committee apparatus to exclude him from the medical staff. [*Memorial Hospital for McHenry County v. Shadur*, 664 F.2d 1058 (7th Cir. 1981)]

Some federal courts have permitted discovery of peer review committee records when violation of a federal constitutional right is alleged. For example, when a female physician requested access to peer review records to prove that a hospital had violated federal law by sexual discrimination, a federal court allowed access despite a state law mandating absolute confidentiality of peer review records. [*Dorsten v. Lapeer County General Hospital*, 88 F.R.D. 583 (E. D. Mich. 1980)] In another case involving a constitutional claim—denial of due process in rejection of an application for privileges in a public hospital—a federal court in Kentucky ruled that the peer review committee records were discoverable even though a state statute specifically prohibited discovery of such records. [*Ott. v. St. Luke Hospital of Campbell County, Inc.*, 522 F. Supp. 706 (E.D. Ky. 1981)]

Q.6:61 What do the courts say about admissibility of committee records?

While courts generally adhere to liberal rules of discovery in the absence of nondiscovery statutes, they are inclined to find hospital and medical staff quality assurance committee records inadmissible as hearsay. Unlike medical records, committee minutes and reports often do not meet the formal requirements of the business records exception to the hearsay rule. Hospital committees do not generate records at or reasonably soon after the time at which the events discussed occurred. Moreover, committee records usually contain conclusions or opinions that generally are inadmissible.

A party who is unable to overcome these barriers to admissibility still may be able to have committee records admitted into evidence under rules of evidence that allow an expert witness to express an opinion based, in part, on information "perceived by or made known to him at or before hearing." [Fed. R. Evid. 703]. If counsel succeeds in obtaining the records and allows the expert witness to review them before trial, that witness may be able to testify concerning the contents of medical records even though the records are found to have been admitted improperly. [Roach, W., ed. 1994,

Medical Records and the Law, Second Edition. (Gaithersburg, MD: Aspen Publishers, Inc.), 193–194]

Q.6:62 What should an internal hospital policy include to protect credentialing information?

An internal hospital policy should be drafted to describe how credential files are to be maintained and accessed. Objectives of this policy should be clearly stated and should address the need to include only the following:

- information that is relevant and material to the credentialing/ reappointment process
- information that ensures the protection of the health professional's rights
- information that provides assurance to patients and regulatory agencies that professionals delivering care are well qualified

Depending on state law, the hospital may wish to maintain two separate files for each health care professional. The first file contains only that information necessary for privileges and appointments/ reappointments. This file would be accessible to those persons who discharge official medical staff duties as they relate to the appointment/reappointment and privilege delineation to professional staff. The second file contains information protected (or protectable) under state law that relates to quality assurance, risk management, or peer review activities. Written references, including the department chairman's review form, should be included in this file. The policy should clearly dictate who has access to each type of file and under what circumstances. The circumstances under which a professional can review his or her own file also should be addressed.

The policy also should clearly state that the file is never to leave the office where it is housed, that it should be reviewed in the presence of a representative from the medical staff or professional office, and that at no time should copies of the file be made or alterations made to the original file.

Some state laws require that specific security measures be implemented, such as locked cabinets.

INFORMATION CONTAINED IN SEPARATE CREDENTIAL FILES

Discoverable Credentials File

- letter appointing the professional to the staff
- application processing checklist
- application
- privilege delineation form
- proof of insurance
- copy of license(s)
- American Medical Association form
- curriculum vitae
- miscellaneous items

Nondiscoverable Items for Second File

- quality assurance review forms
- department chair review form
- professional reference questionnaires
- all information regarding legal involvement
- faculty reappointment form (if one is used)
- National Practitioner Data Bank information
- professional liability insurance experience questionnaire
- all information regarding disciplinary action
- any type of negative information about the professional

[*A Quality Assurance Program for Credentialing, Reappointment, and Privilege Delineation of Health Care Professionals: The Risk Manager's Desk Reference*, Runberg and Youngberg, eds. (Gaithersburg, MD: Aspen Publishers, Inc., 1994), 127]

Q.6:63 What should a hospital consider when creating policies regarding peer review committee records?

Since state statutes and court decisions on protection of peer review and quality assurance activities from discovery vary considerably, hospitals should review carefully and understand thoroughly the applicable law. Institutions should organize and operate peer review and quality assurance activities in a manner designed to obtain the greatest possible protection available. While arguments may be made in support of the discoverability of committee records, hospitals generally can operate with greater flexibility and efficiency and with less risk if peer review and quality assurance records carry some degree of protection.

Once the hospital has developed its policies for committee records, all hospital and medical staff personnel involved in committee activities should be educated as to the importance of following those policies meticulously. Peer review and quality assurance activities should be identified as such and documented in a manner that reinforces their official peer review status and is, thereby, likely to qualify them for maximum protection under state law.

All peer review committee minutes and reports should be prepared carefully and should demonstrate that the hospital performed an objective, considered review. In most states, committee minutes should document primarily actions taken on the matter discussed and not the details of the actual discussion or personal comments made by committee members. The hospital should limit distribution of and access to committee minutes and reports to as few individuals and files as possible.

In all matters relating to developing policies on the creation and use of peer review and quality assurance materials, hospitals should consult with their legal counsel, especially in states in which rules of discoverability are ambiguous or in which courts have construed protection statutes narrowly. Hospitals should instruct counsel to advise them of changes in applicable laws as they occur and to review these policies at least annually.

[Roach, W., ed. 1994, *Medical Records and the Law, Second Edition.* (Gaithersburg, MD: Aspen Publishers, Inc.), 194–195]

7

Special Issues for Managed Care Organizations

Most of the material contained in previous sections of this book applies to managed care organizations (MCOs) as well as to hospitals. This section focuses on MCO-specific issues.

Q.7:1 What is managed care?

Managed care is the process of structuring or restructuring a system of financing, purchasing, delivering, measuring, and documenting a broad range of services and products generally referred to as "health care services." There are various organizations involved in this "process" called managed care, which continue to evolve as the health care delivery system evolves. MCOs include HMOs, PPOs, Exclusive Provider Organizations (EPOs), and a number of hybrids of these more familiar models. There are a variety of other entities that participate in managed care as well.

Q.7:2 What are some of the MCOs and other entities involved in managed care?

Health Maintenance Organizations (HMOs) are organized health care systems that are responsible for both the financing and the delivery of a broad range of comprehensive health services to an enrolled population. An HMO can be viewed as a combination of a health insurer and a health care delivery system. HMOs are responsible for arranging for the provision of health care services to their covered members through affiliated providers. HMOs must, therefore, ensure that those members have access to covered health care services. HMOs are also responsible for assuring the quality and appropriateness of the health services they provide to their members. HMO members must have their health care needs met within the HMO system and, generally, cannot opt out of the system and receive reimbursement for care rendered.

The five common models of HMOs are staff, group practice, network, IPA, and direct contract. The primary differences among these models are based on how the HMO relates to its participating physicians.

Preferred Provider Organizations (PPOs) are entities through which employer health benefit plans and health insurance carriers contract to purchase health care services for covered beneficiaries from a selected group of participating providers. Participating providers agree to abide by the PPO's utilization management program and to accept the PPO's reimbursement schedule. The PPO provides incentives to covered individuals to use the participating providers rather than go outside the PPO panel. Covered individuals can choose to go outside the PPO panel but must consequently pay higher copay and deductibles.

Exclusive Provider Organizations (EPOs) are similar to PPOs in organization and purpose but require that their beneficiaries receive all health care services from the EPO providers. This type of organization is not as widespread because of the severe limitations it places on provider choice. A few large employers have used EPOs as a way of controlling costs.

An **Integrated Delivery System (IDS)** is an organization or group of affiliated organizations that provides a full range of hospital and physician services to patients. An IDS may provide home health, hospice, skilled nursing, rehabilitation, and other services.

A **Physician–Hospital Organization (PHO)** is a legal entity consisting of a joint venture of physicians and a hospital. It is formed primarily to facilitate managed care contracting. PHOs may provide credentialing, utilization review, quality assurance, billing, and management information system services, or any combination of those services. The legal structures vary. A PHO aligns physician and hospital incentives.

A **Management Services Organization (MSO)** generally provides the services offered by a PHO but may offer additional services, such as purchase of equipment and supplies, physician office management, and leasing of equipment and office space. MSOs generally provide services to M.D.s, but may also provide services to hospitals.

Q.7:3 Are the reasons for performing credentialing the same for MCOs as for hospitals?

MCOs share with hospitals the goals of providing high quality services and reducing organizational liability. Careful and thorough credentialing is an important element in reaching those goals. The MCO, no matter what the organizational structure, seeks to include only those providers who will render good medical care. The credentialing process will help the MCO determine which providers are suitable to become participating providers in the plan. Contracting with providers who meet all of the credentialing standards is one method of reducing potential liability for the conduct of a participating provider. If there is a solid credentialing program that is integrated effectively with an ongoing quality assessment program, it will assist the MCO to identify and screen out incompetent physicians and help shield the MCO from liability for their negligence. A strong, consistently applied credentialing program will also provide a record of fairness and objectivity to counter provider challenges that they have been denied participation unfairly. For many MCOs, such as PHOs and PPOs, credentialing is not (yet) required by statute or regulation. HMOs, on the other hand, may be required by state HMO law to perform some level of credentialing.

In addition to those concerns and responsibilities, MCOs are under economic pressure to perform credentialing. Payers expect MCOs to have cost-effective, good quality provider panels or networks. From a contracting standpoint, an MCO is better able to position itself to win a contract if it can demonstrate effective provider performance. While there are many elements necessary to do this, including physician profiling, effective quality assurance (QA) and utilization review (UR) programs, and other considerations, the credentialing process is also one of the pivotal elements in demonstrating and maintaining good quality participating providers.

Q.7:4 Are MCOs legally responsible for credentialing and peer review?

Beginning with the *Darling* case in 1965, the courts have clearly established that hospitals have a direct responsibility for the quality of care provided by independent staff members. Failure to meet this responsibility is referred to as corporate negligence. To fulfill its corporate duty, a hospital must carefully select the physicians it permits to practice medicine there and must monitor the care they provide.

The doctrine of corporate negligence is applicable to managed care entities as well. An essential element of managed care is selecting for participation in the managed care system only those who will provide cost-effective, appropriate patient care. If the MCO is making choices among providers (a choice generally left up to the patient in an indemnity insurance environment) and requiring or strongly encouraging enrollees to see only those providers, the MCO has a duty to select those providers carefully and to monitor their performance. Whatever type of MCO is involved, the more that MCO limits covered persons' choices of providers, the greater the risk of liability for negligent credentialing.

The doctrine of *respondeat superior* clearly applies to staff model HMOs in which the HMO employs the physicians and provides the facility within which they offer care. The situation is directly analogous to that of an acute care hospital. When considering IPA model HMOs and PPOs, the circumstances are somewhat different because the patient is not physically "on the premises" of the entity and the IPA model HMO/PPO probably does not employ the physician. The corporate negligence doctrine may nonetheless be applied to those models because of the HMO's or PPO's role in selecting the providers who will participate in the plan and restricting the patients'choice.

Q.7:5 What have the courts held regarding MCOs' legal responsibility for credentialing and peer review?

In a Missouri case, a court considered application of the corporate negligence doctrine to an HMO. [*Harrel v. Total Health Care, Inc.,* 1989 WL 153066 (Mo. App.), *aff'd*, 781 S.W.2d 58 (Mo. 1989)] The appeals court recognized that the HMO had no direct involvement in patient care but, nonetheless, found that it had breached its corporate duty. Because the HMO limited members' choice to the physicians it had selected, there was an unreasonable risk of harm to those enrollees if the HMO selected unqualified or incompetent physicians, the court reasoned. The court concluded that the HMO had a duty to conduct a reasonable investigation of the physicians' credentials and community reputation.

Similarly, a Pennsylvania court ruled that an IPA model HMO had a nondelegable duty to select and retain only competent primary care physicians. [*McClellan v. HMO of Pa.* 604 A.2d 1053 (Pa Super. 1992)] A patient chose a primary care physician from the list of participating providers and went to him for the removal of a mole on her back. Although the patient had informed the physician that the mole recently had undergone a marked change in size and color, the physician discarded the mole without obtaining a biopsy or other histological exam. As a result, the patient's malignant melanoma was not timely diagnosed or treated, and she subsequently died. Her family sued the HMO on several grounds, including negligent selection of the physician.

The court held that the HMO had a duty to select and monitor physicians properly, but it did not base this conclusion on a theory of corporate negligence. Instead, it relied on common law principles that impose liability if one undertakes to render services to another and injures that person through failure to exercise reasonable care. Liability will attach if the failure to exercise reasonable care increases the risk of harm or if the harm is suffered because of the other's reliance on the undertaking.

According to the court, in a case against an IPA model HMO on this basis, the injured party must show that:

- The HMO has undertaken to provide services to the subscriber that the HMO should recognize as necessary for the protection of the member.
- The HMO failed to use reasonable care in selecting, retaining, and/or evaluating the primary care physician.
- The risk of harm to the subscriber was increased as a result of the HMO's failure to use reasonable care.

Typically, state laws governing preferred provider arrangements do not establish credentialing requirements. Although HMO statutes and regulations may require the HMO to maintain such a system, they usually are not prescriptive as to its contents.

Q.7:6 What are the National Committee for Quality Assurance (NCQA) credentialing requirements?

The market trend is to require the NCQA or other accreditation of the MCO as a stamp of approval/indicia of quality. Employer's benefits consultants are increasingly including accreditation questions in requests for proposals for large employers.

NCQA standards require:

- maintenance of written policies and procedures for the credentialing and recredentialing of physicians and dentists every two years according to the policies and procedures adopted by the MCO's governing body and implemented through a designated credentialing committee
- formal review and approval of the credentialing policies and procedures
- designation of a credentialing committee or other peer review body to make recommendations regarding credentialing decisions

- conducting credentialing of, at a minimum, all physicians and other licensed independent practitioners listed in the MCO's member literature
- obtaining, at a minimum, information from primary sources verifying applicant's license
- Drug Enforcement Agency (DEA) or controlled dangerous substances (CDS) certificate, where applicable
- graduation from medical school, residency training, board certification, as applicable
- professional work history
- adequate malpractice insurance
- professional liability claims history
- good standing at the hospital designated as the primary admitting facility
- obtaining a statement by the applicant as to disciplinary activity, physical and mental status, license history, criminal record, lack of impairment, and the correctness and completeness of the application
- requesting information from the NPDB and the state board of medical examiners, and as to Medicare and Medicaid sanctions
- using an appraisal process including member complaints, quality review results, utilization management records, and member satisfaction surveys
- visiting each primary care physician's office to review the site and the physician's recordkeeping
- maintaining written policies and procedures for the initial quality assessment of health delivery organizations with which it intends to contract
- establishing a process for periodic verification of credentials
- maintaining a written description of delegated activities and the delegate's accountability
- maintaining a mechanism for suspension, reduction, or termination of participation of providers, including a reporting mechanism and appellate process.

Q.7:7 Do MCOs do their own credentialing?

It appears that MCOs are moving toward performing their own credentialing functions, although there is still a lot of delegation of that duty taking place. HMOs may delegate credentialing responsibility to a medical group or an IPA, or may rely on hospital credentialing of their providers. Self-funded employers may delegate credentialing of the panels to which they steer their employees to the broker of the provider network, which could be a provider-sponsored entity, an insurer, an HMO, or some other independent entity. If the MCO has delegated certain credentialing functions to the hospital, the MCO will be involved in creating credentialing criteria.

According to the American Accreditation Program, Inc. (AAPI), if a PPO relies on hospital credentialing, it will be downgraded in the AAPI accreditation report. NCQA standards require a written description of the delegated activities and the delegate's accountability for these activities. The MCO must retain the right to approve new providers and sites, and to terminate or suspend individual providers. In addition, the MCO must monitor the effectiveness of the delegate's credentialing and reappointment or recertification processes at least annually. [CR 15.0 (1994)]

There are a number of reasons not to rely on hospital credentialing.

- Checking with several hospitals where the provider has privileges may result in inconsistent reports.
- A hospital may not have disciplined a physician simply because of the time and money it would take to do so, but the physician is not a provider who should be included in the MCO.
- The MCO will still be liable for the credentialing decision even if it relies on a hospital's credentialing.
- If a hospital reveals credentialing information, it may lose its status as privileged information. However, many state laws can be interpreted to permit communication between protected peer review entities. In addition, the NCQA requires that the delegator assess this information in its audits of the delegatee's performance.

Q.7:8 If an MCO decides to delegate its credentialing responsibility, what should it consider in its contract with the credentialing entity?

An MCO may want to consider contract provisions:

- retaining the right to approve new providers or sites and to terminate or suspend individual providers
- requiring indemnification from the credentialing entity for losses attributable to negligence in the credentialing process
- ensuring that the credentialing entity carries insurance coverage that extends to errors or omissions in credentialing
- requiring the MCO to be named as an additional insured

Q.7:9 Who approves the credentialing policies and procedures?

The governing body or the group or individual to whom the governing body had delegated the credentialing function approves the credentialing policies and procedures. The function may be delegated to the quality assessment committee or a credentialing committee, or to the CEO or chief medical officer.

Q.7:10 Are the credentialing criteria the same for an MCO as for an acute care facility?

Many of the criteria, for example, clinical competence, ability to work with others, and board certification, that apply in the hospital setting are also applicable to MCOs. Because practitioners in many MCOs operate from their own office locations, the MCO may have very specific criteria relating to evaluation of the physician's office practice.

These criteria may include office inspection to evaluate the physician's office practice as far as adequate facilities (meet ADA accessibility standards), maintenance of office equipment, efficient operation (adequate hours of coverage, recordkeeping, etc.), and technician requirements, where applicable.

Alan Bloom, Senior Vice President, General Counsel of Maxicare Health Plans, Inc., indicates that MCOs must have criteria that ensure that health care professionals provide services that are available, accessible, and acceptable. According to Bloom, staffing patterns of contracting medical groups and the services available should be monitored. [Alan Bloom, *Physician Credentialing in Managed Care*, ANNALS OF HEALTH LAW, VOL. I (1992)]

The criteria of economic practice patterns are, if anything, even more vital in an MCO setting. The MCO may have specific criteria related to patient average length of stay and cost per case. If the MCO is going to make participation decisions based on economic criteria, it must have the data to back up its decisions. This is necessary to ensure fairness and prevent allegations of anticompetitive motives for exclusion decisions.

Q.7:11 How is credentialing done in integrated delivery systems?

Because integrated delivery systems are fairly new in the health care arena and are still evolving, credentialing is still done largely on a facility-by-facility basis. There is recognition in the industry, however, that centralization and integration of credentialing and peer review in integrated delivery systems is a desirable goal. [See, e.g., Lowell C. Brown, *New "Mental Models" for Credentialing and Peer Review*, HEALTH SYSTEMS REVIEW, (May/June 1994).] According to Brown, centralization of these activities will reduce or eliminate duplication in both credentialing and medical staff discipline. Instead of applying for separate privileges at several facilities in the same system or network, a practitioner would apply to all of them at once. In the present decentralized system, if a practitioner's privileges are reduced at one facility, that practitioner still retains similar privileges at another facility in the same network, necessitating numerous hearings. A centralized model would require only one disciplinary hearing.

Q.7:12 What is economic credentialing and why is it particularly pertinent in a managed care environment?

Economic credentialing is the use of economic criteria in making credentialing decisions. The goal of MCOs is to provide quality health care cost effectively. A provider who consistently overutilizes or underutilizes resources is endangering both aspects of that goal. A provider who consistently overutilizes resources may not be providing quality care because that provider may be rendering unnecessary care, e.g., unnecessary surgery or laboratory tests, or care delivered at an inappropriate level, e.g., inpatient rather than outpatient. In addition, the provider who overutilizes resources is endangering the cost-effective operation of the MCO. A provider who consistently underutilizes resources also may be providing less than quality care. While such conduct initially may seem more cost effective, it is a false economy. A provider who is not rendering medically necessary care eventually will be sued for malpractice. The MCO may share in that liability.

Q.7:13 Have there been any cases that address economic credentialing?

There have been a few cases that directly address economic factors. *Rosenblum v. Tallahassee Memorial Regional Medical Center, Inc.*, is considered to be the first pure economic credentialing case. In that case, a thoracic surgeon sued when he was denied open heart surgery privileges at a hospital. The physician was the director of the open heart surgery program at a competing hospital and was publicly supportive of that program. The court held that the hospital that denied him privileges could properly consider economic factors as well as medical factors in making a determination on granting clinical privileges. It cautioned, however, that while economic considerations are valid, they must not be arbitrary. The court noted that the physician was very highly qualified in a rare specialty that rarely is used. It concluded that the hospital's decision to deny privileges was reasonable because it otherwise would have incurred substantial cost to establish and equip a department where the physician could exercise those privileges. [No. 91-589 (Fla. Cir. Ct., June 22, 1992)]

The *Rosenblum* case was based largely on a Florida statute that establishes factors a medical staff must take into consideration in making credentialing recommendations to the governing board and sets out the criteria for eligibility for staff membership the governing board must use. [Fla. Stat. §395.011(5)] That law lists the various criteria, then adds, "and by such other elements as may be determined by the governing board." The court ruled that this provision embraces the concept of economic credentialing.

In another managed care case, a federal court upheld the termination of two allergists who had failed to practice in a cost-effective manner. The court explicitly approved the use of participation decisions based on utilization patterns. [*Hassan v. Independent Practice Association*, 698 F.Supp. 679 (E.D. Mich. 1988)]

Q.7:14 How is the peer review process documented in an MCO?

The peer review process is documented in the quality assurance plan and the credentialing plan. In nonstaff model MCOs, providers generally are bound by contractual obligations rather than by medical staff bylaws. A participating provider that signs a contract with an MCO agrees to be bound by the MCO's policies, including the peer review procedures delineated in the quality assurance plan and the credentialing plan. Passing and maintaining credentialing status routinely is a condition precedent to obtaining and maintaining the contractual relationship.

Q.7:15 What kind of committees are there in an MCO?

This varies from state to state and from MCO to MCO. There are fewer committees in MCOs than in hospitals. HMOs generally have a separate credentials plan, a separate QA plan, and a separate UR plan. This is generally the case because of the requirements of state regulators and the preferences of payers and employers who may contract with the MCO. There may be a separate committee related to each of these areas. Some HMOs, however, have an umbrella committee that has oversight over all of these areas.

Many times, MCO committees will be analogous to hospital committees in function but will have different names. For example, the committee that performs the QA function may be called the medical management committee, and the committee performing the credentialing function may be called the provider committee.

Q.7:16 What is the advantage of having an umbrella committee?

This may be desirable from a risk management perspective. When the committees are functioning independently, it is possible for a provider to be under review in one area and passed over in another. With an umbrella committee that performs or oversees all of the functions, this would not happen. There is general oversight and knowledge of the whole picture with regard to particular providers.

Q.7:17 Who is on MCO committees?

Committees are generally composed of community participating physicians as well as members of the MCO management.

Q.7:18 How do complaints about a provider come to the attention of an MCO?

Complaints about providers may come from many different sources. For example, a referral can be made to QA as a result of a member complaint. A complaint can come from an employer, a broker, another provider, an MCO employee—almost anyone can make a complaint that could result in a referral to an MCO QA committee. The appropriate committee must then decide whether to formally investigate the complaint.

Q.7:19 Are the due process requirements the same in MCOs as in hospitals when participation rights are affected?

In the MCO context, physicians generally do not have the same procedural rights as are afforded by hospitals in making credentialing decisions. By establishing a basic fair process scheme, however, an MCO will:

- provide objective standards as criteria for making credentialing decisions
- satisfy physicians' expectations of fair process created by their hospital experiences
- establish a record of fair treatment should an excluded or disciplined physician contest a decision in court.

Basic fair process includes notice and an opportunity to be heard, which need not be elaborate procedures in the MCO context. Some health law attorneys indicate that an opportunity to be heard need not mean a hearing but could be met by establishing a process whereby the excluded provider can correct the record in writing. If there is a hearing, it need not include the full spectrum of constitutional safeguards, such as a right to counsel. The final credentialing decision, however, should not be made by the applicant's direct economic competitors. [See Doug Hastings, PHO, NHLA Annual Meeting, 1994.]

If the MCO wants to avail itself of the protections available under the HCQIA, however, it will have to afford practitioners the due process measures mandated by that law. As suggested by Hastings, (see above cite), an MCO may want to have two separate fair process procedures. When the issue involves a matter of competence or professional conduct, the practitioner would be entitled to the procedures outlined in HCQIA, thereby bringing the MCO within that law's immunity provisions. When the credentialing decision does not pertain to professional competence or conduct and the HCQIA immunities are, therefore, not available, the procedure may involve simply notice and an opportunity to be heard.

Once an MCO decides to incorporate fair process into its credentialing program, that process should be spelled out clearly and followed consistently.

Q.7:20 Is peer review in an MCO the same as peer review in a hospital?

It is very difficult to make generalizations about peer review in MCOs because there are so many different types. An MCO that is based on IPA agreements or network agreements may operate very differently from an open-access fee-for-service HMO that has individual provider agreements or a staff model HMO.

How peer review is conducted in any particular MCO may be determined by a number of factors, including the requirements and immunities of the state peer review law, the market conditions and geographical area, and the leverage of the MCO.

The MCO develops its Quality Assessment Plan, which contains the peer review process. It will do so by taking into consideration whether the state peer review law will afford it some protections if various elements are included. It will also take into consideration the immunities under the federal HCQIA if certain procedures are followed.

When an MCO negotiates contracts with providers, complying with the QA plan is part of the provider's obligation under the contract. Although many aspects of the contract may be negotiable, the QA plan is not. It would be unmanageable to have different procedures available to different providers. In addition, in the case of HMOs, many state HMO laws require that the QA plan be approved by the state regulator. Once it is approved, it cannot be arbitrarily altered.

Market conditions and provider culture differ in various geographic areas. While an MCO in one area might be able to have a peer review process that does not contain a hearing requirement, that might be totally unacceptable to providers in another area, and the MCO would not be able to attract or retain providers without including a right to a hearing.

The amount of leverage an MCO has in a particular geographic area might also dictate how the peer review process is structured. If participation in an MCO is considered very desirable by providers in a certain area, the MCO may have more latitude in structuring its peer review process.

Q.7:21 How does an investigation begin and proceed?

Generally, the QA committee (or the committee performing that function) determines that a complaint is legitimate and should trigger an investigation. The MCO administrative staff then gathers the necessary materials and information. This may involve obtaining records from the provider's office. Provider agreements contain provisions that require the provider to cooperate with and participate in all credentialing, quality assurance, and utilization review programs.

If the investigation reveals a problem, the QA committee will assign it a severity level. These vary from plan to plan. As an example, severity level one might be a problem that does not indicate the possibility of patient injury. Severity level three may be a problem that indicates a high possibility of patient injury. The severity level will guide the committee in determining what action it will pursue.

The severity level as well as the possible discipline for each severity level is spelled out in the QA plan. MCOs attempt to provide the QA committee as much flexibility as possible as far as what kind of discipline can be imposed for each level of severity. The level of creativity available to the committee will depend on the wording of the QA plan.

Many times, the discipline will consist of education or counseling but can consist of various measures, including expulsion of the provider from the plan.

If the QA plan indicates that the right to a hearing is triggered, the provider should receive notice of the charges and should be given an opportunity to respond. Depending on how the MCO has structured the provider appeal process, the committee may appoint a hearing officer, who may be an independent attorney who is familiar with MCO matters. The MCO may also refer the matter to a separate appeals committee.

Q.7:22 Do all disciplinary actions have to go through the credentials committee?

That varies with each MCO. Having all disciplinary actions go through the credentials committee could become cumbersome. For example, the QA committee may be investigating a particular matter and determine what it considers to be an appropriate corrective action. That committee is composed of various community physicians. If the matter must then be shifted to the credentials committee, another group of community physicians would be reviewing the same information and be making the decision. The MCO may want to empower the QA committee to go forward with the disciplinary action and have the credentials committee become involved only on appeal or have the QA committee refer the matter directly to a broader oversight committee for appellate action. How these procedures are structured will vary with the needs of each MCO and what works well in a given area.

Q.7:23 Are providers in MCOs entitled to an appeal from a corrective action plan decision?

Whether practitioners in MCOs are entitled to an appeal from a corrective action plan depends on what is stated in the QA plan. In some plans, an appeal is at the discretion of the MCO, while other plans routinely provide an appeals process. The NCQA standards require that there be an appeal process for instances where the MCO chooses to reduce, suspend, or terminate a practitioner's privileges. [CR 14.2 (1994)]

Some contracts contain provisions requiring the exhaustion of internal administrative remedies, and most MCO contracts contain binding arbitration clauses. Therefore, if a provider is subjected to corrective action to which he or she objects and there is an appeals mechanism, the provider must appeal. If the provider is dissatisfied with the outcome of the appeal, he or she must submit the dispute to binding arbitration.

Q.7:24 Can an MCO terminate a physician under an employment contract without a hearing?

If an MCO has a quality of care issue with a provider, the MCO is better off addressing that problem directly through the established fair hearing plan. This is true for several reasons.

- If contract termination is used as an "out" in most situations, this will become apparent to practitioners, payers, employers, and regulators. The MCO will then lose credibility.
- If a terminated practitioner subsequently sues, charging that the termination was in violation of the antitrust laws, the MCO may have to admit the real reason for termination. At that point, it has lost the protection of the HCQIA because it has not granted a fair hearing.
- If an MCO is aware of quality of care problems but simply terminates without cause, a patient who is subsequently injured by the practitioner may sue the MCO for failing to carry out a corporate duty.

Whether the quality problem was reportable will depend on the circumstances. If it was reportable and the MCO failed to do so, it may be subject to civil monetary penalties.

Q.7:25 Are there any special considerations in a staff model HMO setting?

The physician contract should be coordinated with the fair hearing plan. If a provider is terminated, that provider should be entitled to only one hearing. The bylaws should state that medical staff privileges are terminated if the provider is excluded from the HMO. There should not be a hearing regarding termination from the HMO, then another hearing in order to revoke medical staff privileges.

Q.7:26 Who approves the exclusion or participation of practitioners in the MCO?

The MCO committee performing the credentialing function makes its recommendations to the board or to a committee of the board charged with this responsibility. The board will approve contract status, decline to contract, or return the matter to the credentials committee for further clarification.

Q.7:27 Are there antitrust implications in excluding physicians from an MCO?

Providers who are not accepted as participating providers in an MCO may allege that the exclusion constituted a group boycott in violation of the antitrust laws. To establish a group boycott, there must be more than one actor, anticompetitive intent or the absence of legitimate reasons for the conduct, and a certain degree of market power.

Control is an important issue in this context. If the plan is provider-controlled, that raises the question whether the decision to exclude actually was made by a group of competitors, not by the MCO. In one case, for example, a court found that several competing hospitals controlled the board of a Blue Cross association and were the parties actually making the exclusionary decisions. That constituted an illegal group boycott. In a nonprovider-controlled plan, there is less risk that competitors will be making such decisions and, therefore, less likelihood of a successful group boycott charge. [*St. Bernard General Hospital, Inc. v. Hospital Services Association of New Orleans, Inc.*, 712 F.2d 978 (5th Cir. 1983), *cert. denied*, 466 U. S. 970 (1984)]

Even if there is an agreement among competitors to exclude a provider, however, the actors must have significant market power before the conduct will be considered per se illegal. If the actors do not have significant market power, the conduct will be analyzed under the rule of reason to establish whether the conduct constituted an illegal restraint of trade. That will be determined by balancing the competitive and anticompetitive effects of the conduct. In one case, a court held that an HMO that refused to allow a radiology group to participate in the HMO did not violate the antitrust laws because the conduct had no anticompetitive effect. It held that even if there had been a conspiracy to exclude the group, there was no antitrust violation because the IPA and HMO had insufficient market power to restrain trade. [*Capital Imaging Associates v. Mohawk Valley Medical Associates, Inc.*, 791 F. Supp. 956 (N.D. N.Y. 1992)]

Q.7:28 Do NPDB reporting requirements apply to MCOs?

"Health care entities," as defined in the HCQIA, must report adverse actions against privileges. "Health care entity" is defined as an entity that "provides health care services and that follows a formal peer review process for the purpose of furthering quality health care." [42 U.S.C. §11151 (4) (A) (ii)] If an MCO falls within this definition, it has reporting responsibilities.

HMOs are considered health care entities under the HCQIA and, therefore, have reporting requirements. PPOs, on the other hand, generally are seen as arranging health care services rather than providing health care services. Under this perception, it would not have reporting responsibilities. The perception would apply to PHOs as well. While the same argument might be made for certain models, there is no distinction made in the statute.

Q.7:29 Are MCOs required to query the NPDB?

HMOs are required to query the NPDB. Other types of MCOs are not required to do so. State law may impose such a requirement. Accreditation standards that require NPDB inquiries may eventually be used to set a standard of care in the future.

Q.7:30 Do HCQIA immunities apply to MCOs?

If an MCO is engaged in "professional review action," as defined in the HCQIA, it will be entitled to that law's protection from liability as long as it meets the procedural requirements outlined in the law. A professional review action must be based on the "competence or professional conduct of an individual physician . . . ." [42 U.S.C. §11151 (a)]

Q.7:31   What options do MCOs have for contracting with the federal government under the Medicare/Medicaid programs?

Medicare contracting

There are three major methods of managed care Medicare contracting: Medicare risk contracts, Medicare cost contracts, and Medicare demonstration projects.

Medicare risk contracts.   Federally qualified HMOs and competitive medical plans can contract with the government on a prepaid basis. A competitive medical plan is essentially an HMO that does not meet the federal qualification requirements. The statute and regulations governing Medicare risk contracts require that the entity be fiscally sound, maintain an adequate and accessible delivery system, establish a satisfactory quality assurance program, and implement a grievance procedure. This program also contains minimum enrollment requirements, open enrollment mandates, and must have no more than 50 percent Medicare/Medicaid enrollees.

Medicare cost contracts.   The federal government can enter into cost-based contracts with HMOs. Under this type of contract, HMOs are paid for the costs they incur in serving a Medicare population. There are Section 1876 cost contracts, which must meet many of the requirements that must be met for a risk contract, and there are Section 1833 contracts, also known as health care prepayment plans, which have fewer requirements than Section 1876 cost contracts.

Medicare demonstration projects.   There are several demonstration projects that present contracting opportunities for MCOs. The three major projects are the Medicare insured group (MIG) demonstration, the Medicare SELECT demonstration, and a partial risk-sharing demonstration in areas of high HMO penetration.

Medicaid contracting

There are three major models operating under the Medicaid program: comprehensive risk HMOs, prepaid health plans, and primary care case management.

Comprehensive risk HMO. Comprehensive risk HMOs receive a fixed amount for each individual and, in return, must provide the agreed upon comprehensive set of services. The HMO is "at risk" because an individual may use more services than anticipated, and the HMO will suffer a loss. On the other hand, if the individual uses fewer services than anticipated, the HMO could make a profit. HMOs may also enter into Medicaid contracts in which they assume partial or no risk.

Prepaid health plans (PHPs). A prepaid health plan is an entity that contracts with a Medicaid agency to provide medical services to Medicaid beneficiaries but does not qualify as an HMO. PHPs can enter into nonrisk and noncomprehensive contracts but cannot enter into risk comprehensive contracts.

Primary care case management programs (PCCMPs). PCCMPs are managed care programs that have obtained a freedom of choice waiver and receive payment on a fee-for-service basis. Medicaid beneficiaries can select a primary care physician responsible for providing primary care and authorizing specialty care. In addition to the fee for service, the provider is paid a nominal case management fee.

Q.7:32 What are the credentialing implications of contracting with the government under Medicare/Medicaid?

MCOs that contract with the government are subject to numerous requirements, including statutory or regulatory provisions regarding quality assessment, peer review, and/or credentialing. The requirements vary depending on the model.

8

Clinical Practice Guidelines

Q.8:1 What is a clinical practice guideline?

Clinical practice guidelines, also called "practice parameters," "protocols", "critical pathways," "practice policies," "care maps," and many other terms, are an attempt to set out objective statements of the essential clinical choices that should be made in treating a particular medical disease or condition. Clinical practice guidelines may be adopted as criteria for the delineation of clinical privileges.

Part of the mandate of the federal Agency for Health Care Policy and Research is the development and periodic review and updating of treatment-specific or condition-specific guidelines. [42 U.S.C. §1320b-12(a)(1)(B)] The intent is to use such practice guidelines to improve the efficiency and effectiveness of the Medicare and Medicaid programs. The cost and effort necessary to develop practice parameters, however, is immense. As of 1994, the agency had published fewer than a dozen guidelines.

In addition to governmental efforts, single specialty professional organizations are also involved in the development of clinical practice guidelines. Private entities have also begun to develop guidelines. There are, as of 1994, over 1,500 guidelines established by various groups.

Q.8:2 Who decides which clinical practice guidelines, if any, should be used?

The credentials committee of the medical staff should have the responsibility of investigating whether specific clinical practice guidelines should be adopted. There should be written criteria determining what factors the committee will use to make such decisions. The credentials committee then makes its recommendation to the medical executive committee, which, in turn, makes its recommendation to the governing body for its review and approval.

Q.8:3 Who must be informed that the governing body has approved adoption of a clinical practice guideline?

Medical staff members should be notified that the clinical practice guideline has been added to hospital policy. The guideline will then be used as a basis for delineating the clinical privileges of applicants. Clinical practice guidelines should be applied prospectively, not to physicians whose applications are pending when the guideline is adopted. Applicants should be informed of guideline eligibility criteria and be asked to provide documentation that they meet the criteria.

Q.8:4 What happens if physicians who hold privileges when the clinical practice guidelines are adopted do not meet the guideline standards?

The practice parameters should be integrated into the reappointment process in a manner consistent with credentialing policies and bylaws. Physicians who do not meet practice parameter standards can suffer a technical reduction of privileges at reappointment. They may be given an opportunity to voluntarily relinquish those privileges without a hearing. If they do so, there is no NPDB reporting requirement as privileges were not reduced due to quality of care concerns. The facility may decide to phase in the new guideline to give existing staff members an opportunity to comply with the new requirements.

Q.8:5 What are the legal implications of clinical practice guidelines?

The legal issues associated with clinical practice guidelines are just emerging and range from establishing the standard of care for various procedures to payment issues. In the credentialing context, guidelines may be important for a few reasons.

- If a particular guideline is adopted and a practitioner's privileges are adversely affected, the practitioner could sue claiming that the guidelines are inaccurate and negligently adopted. It is, therefore, important that the medical staff thoroughly investigate the guidelines and ensure that they are legitimate and based on credible data.
- If the guideline is used to reduce a practitioner's privileges, he or she may allege that the guideline was applied in an arbitrary manner for anticompetitive purposes. It is important for the facility to apply the guideline requirements in a consistent manner, with no exceptions, such as phase-in period for current staff members, that are not specifically adopted.
- If a clinical practice guideline is adopted and a practitioner fails to meet it, the criterion used for disciplinary action is clear and objective. There should be less chance of the basis for the action to be challenged.
- If there are guidelines available and a hospital does not adopt them, a patient who is injured may allege that the hospital was negligent for *not* adopting a guideline. The hospital should carefully document its reasons for adopting or rejecting particular guidelines.

Appendix A _____

Discoverability and Admissibility of Medical Staff Committee Records

This state-by-state analysis consists of a listing of the applicable statutes and important cases dealing with the discoverability and admissibility of medical staff committee records in each state. The list of cases for each state is not exhaustive, and additional citations may be encountered in legal research. The state-by-state analysis does not constitute an exhaustive treatment of statutory protection in each state.

ALABAMA

Statutory Provisions

Ala. Code §34-24-58.

The decisions, opinions, actions, and proceedings of utilization review committees or committees of similar nature or purpose are privileged if they are rendered, entered, or acted on in good faith and without malice and on the basis of facts reasonably known or reasonably believed to exist.

ALASKA

Statutory Provisions

Alaska Stat. §§18.23.030 and 18.23.070.

All data and information acquired by a review organization in the exercise of its duties shall be held in confidence and shall not be disclosed to anyone except to the extent necessary to carry out the purposes of the review committee. Such data and information are not subject to subpoena or discovery. Records and proceedings of review organizations are not subject to discovery or introduction into evidence in civil actions against health care providers arising out of matters that are the subject of evaluation and review. However, information that is otherwise available from original sources is not immune from discovery and introduction into evidence simply because it was presented to a review committee. In addition, a person whose conduct or competence has been reviewed by a committee may obtain information for purposes of appellate review of the committee's action.

Similarly, discovery proceedings may be brought by a plaintiff who claims that (1) information provided to a review organization was false and (2) the person providing the information knew or had reason to know it was false.

ARIZONA

Statutory Provisions

Ariz. Rev. Stat. §§36-445, 36-445.01, 36-2403, and 36-2917.

All proceedings, records, and materials prepared in connection with committees that review the nature, quality, and necessity of care provided in a hospital and the preventability of complications and deaths occurring in a hospital, including all peer reviews of individual health care providers practicing in and applying to practice in hospitals, and the records of such reviews, are confidential and not subject to discovery. Discovery is allowable in proceedings before the board of medical or osteopathic examiners, in an action by an individual health care provider against a hospital or its staff arising from discipline of that health care provider or refusal, termination, suspension, or limitation of his or her privileges, or in proceedings initiated by state licensing or certification agencies.

Selected Cases

Tucson Medical Center, Inc. v. Misevch, 545 P.2d 958 (Ariz. 1976). Statement and information considered by a medical review committee are subject to subpoena, but reports and minutes of the committee are not.

Samaritan Health Services v. City of Glendale, 714 P.2d 887 (Ariz. Ct. App. 1986). Arizona hospitals have no duty to assert the physician-patient privilege when served with a search warrant for patients' medical records.

John C. Lincoln Hospital and Health Center v. Superior Court of County of Maricopa, 768 P.2d 188 (Ariz. Ct. App. 1989). Minutes of a hospital's trauma critical care committee were protected under the state peer review statute because they concerned operating room communications. A Quality Assurance Program Incident Report was discoverable, however, because it did not constitute discussion, exchange, opinions, or proceedings relating to reviews but only contained factual data.

Yuma Regional Medical Center v. Superior Court of the State of Arizona, No. V-60524 (Ariz Ct. App. April 22, 1993). Arizona's peer review privilege protects the identity of participants in and written items submitted to peer review proceedings from discovery in medical malpractice cases. The peer review privilege does not, however, protect information that originated outside the peer review process and that is discoverable from other sources.

ARKANSAS

Statutory Provisions

Ark. Code Ann. §§20-9-304 and 20-9-503.

All information, interviews, reports, statements, memoranda, and other data used by hospital staff committees and other committees in the course of medical studies, the purpose of which is to reduce morbidity and mortality, and any other findings or conclusions resulting from such studies are privileged and may not be received in evidence in any legal proceeding. This statute does not apply to original medical records pertaining to patients.

The proceedings and records of peer review committees are not subject to discovery and are inadmissible in any civil action against a provider of health services arising out of matters that are the subject of evaluation and review. However, documents, information, and records that are otherwise available from original sources are not protected simply because they were presented during committee proceedings.

Selected Cases

Baxter County Newspapers v. Medical Staff of Baxter General Hospital, 622 S.W.2d 495 (Ark. 1981). The state Freedom of Information Act (FOIA) was held to permit public access to medical review committee proceedings because such proceedings were not expressly exempted from the FOIA.

Hendrickson v. Leipzig, 715 F. Supp. 1443 (E.D. Ark. 1989). Peer review legislation privileges information regarding a hospital's revocation of a physician's medical staff privileges that a hospital provided to the state medical board and cannot be discovered in a patient's malpractice suit.

CALIFORNIA

Statutory Provisions

Cal. Evid. Code §1157.

The proceedings and records of organized medical staff committees, the function of which is to evaluate and improve the quality of care rendered in a hospital, are not subject to discovery. In addition, no person in attendance at a committee meeting can be required to testify as to what transpired there. The prohibition relating to discovery, however, does not apply to statements made by a person who attended such a committee meeting and who is a party to an action or proceeding, the subject of which was reviewed at the meeting, or to any person requesting staff privileges. Other exceptions are noted.

Selected Cases

Matchett v. Superior Court for County of Yuba, 115 Cal. Rptr. 317 (Ct. App. 1974). Reports of various medical staff committees are immune from discovery in a malpractice suit, but records of hospital management administration are discoverable.

Schulz v. Superior Court, 136 Cal. Rptr. 67 (Ct. App. 1977). Discovery of reports of the hospital's medical advisory board was denied in a malpractice action.

Roseville Community Hospital v. Superior Court, 139 Cal. Rptr. 170 (Ct. App. 1977). Statements made by individuals at a committee meeting of the hospital's medical staff are discoverable by persons whose requests for hospital staff privileges were denied.

Henry Mayo Newhall Memorial Hospital v. Superior Court, 146 Cal. Rptr. 542 (Ct. App. 1978). A hospital's filing of the transcript of a staff committee hearing in an unrelated administrative mandamus action does not constitute a waiver of immunity from discovery under §1157 of the California Evidence Code.

County of Kern v. Superior Court, 147 Cal. Rptr. 248 (Ct. App. 1978). The court found the trial court's order granting a discovery motion in a malpractice action to be overbroad and violative of §1157 of the California Evidence Code.

West Covina Hospital v. Superior Court, 200 Cal. Rptr. 162 (Ct. App. 1984). The records and proceedings of a hospital committee are nondiscoverable, even if the physician who provided the care in question was a member of the committee when it was reviewing his or her conduct.

West Covina Hospital v. Superior Court, 226 Cal. Rptr. 132 (Cal. 1986). A committee member may testify voluntarily in court about the proceedings of a hospital medical staff committee meeting, but he or she may not be required or compelled to do so.

Mt. Diablo Hospital Medical Center v. Superior Court, 204 Cal. Rptr. 626 (Ct. App. 1984). The records or proceedings of a hospital committee are nondiscoverable even if needed to hold a hospital accountable for the competency of its medical staff.

Saddleback Community Hospital v. Superior Court, 204 Cal. Rptr. 598 (Ct. App. 1984). Hospital administration records are discoverable to the extent that they do not contain references to nondiscoverable medical staff committee proceedings. Private court review of requested records is necessary to protect immune information from discovery.

Snell v. Superior Court, 204 Cal. Rptr. 200 (Ct. App. 1984). Physician personnel records maintained by a hospital medical review committee are immune from discovery because they are not hospital administration records but are the nondiscoverable records of an organized medical staff committee.

Brown v. Superior Court, 214 Cal. Rptr. 266 (Ct. App. 1985). That a hospital, in fact, screened the competence of a staff physician is discoverable in a malpractice action, although the information contained in that evaluation is protected from disclosure.

Santa Rosa Memorial Hospital v. Superior Court, 220 Cal. Rptr. 236 (Ct. App. 1986). Information concerning whether a patient's treatment was reviewed by an infection control committee is immune from discovery if the hospital can show that such review would not be undertaken as a matter of course because disclosure would indicate a suspicion of dereliction. An infection control committee is considered a medical staff committee for the purposes of the state peer review confidentiality law notwithstanding that the committee is composed of a majority of personnel who are not physicians or medical staff members. Information obtained by hospital administrators, which does not derive from a medical staff committee investigation or evaluation, is not rendered immune from discovery merely because it is later made known to or placed in the possession of a medical staff committee.

Mt. Diablo Hospital District v. Superior Court, 227 Cal. Rptr. 790 (Ct. App. 1986). The minutes of a hospital peer review committee are nondiscoverable even if they pertain to the evaluation and adoption of standards for new treatments and drug care and not to the evaluation of the past performance of physicians.

California Eye Institute v. Superior Court of Fresno County, 264 Cal. Rptr. 83 (Ct. App. 1989). A physician who sued a medical center, alleging that it had wrongfully interfered with his medical staff privileges, could not discover records relating to the restriction of his privileges. Under California law, hospital committee records are immune from discovery, except for a person who is requesting staff privileges. At the time of the suit, the center had reinstated the physician's privileges and he was, therefore, not entitled to the records.

Teasdale v. Marin General Hospital, 138 F.R.D. 696 (N.D. Cal. 1991). A physician who brought an antitrust suit attacking the rescission of hospital surgical privileges was entitled to discover information in the credential files of the physicians he was suing. The peer review committee's decisions with respect to other physicians who allegedly participated in the conspiracy could be the most important evidence in the suit.

People v. Superior Court of California for Los Angeles, 286 Cal. Rptr. 478 (Ct. App. 1991). State legislation granting immunity from discovery to the proceedings of hospital peer review bodies does not provide immunity against discovery in proceedings against a physician for criminal negligence.

Cedars-Sinai Medical Center v. Superior Court, 16 Cal. Rptr. 2d 253 (Cal. Ct. App. 1993). State peer review legislation protects the identities of peer review committee members from discovery.

Alexander v. Superior Court of Los Angeles County, No. B062903 (Cal. Oct. 14, 1993). Medical staff applications and reapplications for privilege fall within the category of "records" and "proceedings" in the state's statutory peer review privilege. The legislation does not distinguish between records generated by a committee and those submitted to a committee, the court concluded.

Willis v. Superior Court of Santa Clara County, No. H011221 (Cal. Ct. App. Nov. 16, 1993). Hospital administrative information generated independently of staff committees'quality of care functions that do not reveal committee activities are not privileged simply because the material is provided to the committees.

COLORADO

Statutory Provisions

Colo. Rev. Stat. §§12-36.5-104 and 25-3-109

The records of professional review committees, utilization review committees, quality control committees, peer review organizations, and governing boards are not subject to subpoena or discovery and may not be introduced into evidence in a civil suit against the physician who is the subject of the records. A separate statute for hospitals states that records, reports, and other information that is part of a quality management program designed to reduce risk of patient injury or improve the quality of patient care are confidential. This information is not subject to subpoena and is not admissible in any civil or administrative proceeding.

Individuals who collected or used the quality management information may not testify regarding the information unless they have independent knowledge of the information or if other exceptions apply.

Selected Cases

Posey v. District Court, 586 P.2d 36 (Colo. 1978). Section 12-43.5-102 of the Colorado Revised Statutes is applicable to civil suits against hospitals as well as physicians.

Davidson v. Light, 79 F.R.D. 137 (D. Colo. 1978). Section 12-43.5-102 is designed to confer immunity on professional review committees, not on hospital infection control committees.

Franco v. District Court, 641 P.2d 922 (Colo. 1982). Records of peer review committees are not discoverable by a physician who seeks to compel a hospital to restore his surgical privileges.

Beth Israel Hospital and Geriatric Center v. District Court, 683 P.2d 343 (Colo. 1984). A physician seeking to compel the restoration of his surgical privileges may discover his patient's records even though they were reviewed by a hospital surgical committee. The records did not become immune from discovery as "records of a review committee" merely because the committee used them in its deliberations.

CONNECTICUT

Statutory Provisions

Conn. Gen. Stat. §19a-17b.

Proceedings of peer review, utilization review, medical audit, and similar committees are not subject to discovery and are not admissible into evidence in any civil action arising out of matters that are the subject of committee evaluation and review, subject to four exceptions. These include writings recorded independently of such proceedings, the testimony of any person concerning facts acquired through personal knowledge and independently of such proceedings, use in any health care provider proceedings concerning the termination or restriction of staff privileges other than peer review, and disclosure in any civil action of the fact that staff privileges were terminated.

Selected Cases

Morse v. Gerity, 520 F. Supp. 470 (D. Conn. 1981). Peer review documents are nondiscoverable regardless of whether they pertain to the subject matter of a lawsuit.

Connecticut Commissioner of Health Services v. William W. Backus Hospital, 485 A.2d 937 (Conn. Super. Ct. 1984). Hospital peer review records may be discovered by the state medical examining board when investigating physician medical misconduct because such investigations are not considered civil actions in which the records would be statutorily privileged.

DELAWARE

Statutory Provisions

Del. Code Ann. tit. 24, §1768.
Records and proceedings of hospital and nursing home quality review committees are confidential, to be used only in the exercise of proper committee functions, not public records, and not available for court subpoena or subject to discovery.

Selected Cases

Register v. Wilmington Medical Center, Inc., 377A.2d 8 (Del. 1977). Staff reports concerning performance of a resident physician are discoverable in a malpractice action.

Robinson v. LeRoy, No. 84-121 (D. Del. Nov. 16, 1984). Records of hospital committees that consider applications for staff privileges are not discoverable in a malpractice action because Delaware's peer review records confidentiality statute extends to the records and proceedings of such committees.

Dworkin v. St. Francis Hospital, Inc., 517 A.2d 302 (Del. Super. Ct. 1986). Peer review committee records pertaining to the termination of a physician's privileges in violation of hospital bylaws are discoverable by the physician because the statutory peer review privilege does not protect improper peer review activities.

DISTRICT OF COLUMBIA

Statutory Provisions

D.C. Code Ann. §32-505.
Absent a showing of extraordinary necessity, the files, records, findings, opinions, recommendations, evaluations, and reports of a peer review committee are not subject to discovery or admissible into evidence in any civil or administrative proceeding, except for the limited purpose of adjudicating the appropriateness of any adverse action affecting a health professional's employment, membership, or association. This privilege does not extend to primary health records or to any oral or written statements submitted to or presented before a committee.

Selected Cases

Laws v. Georgetown University Hospital, 656 F. Supp. 824 (D.D.C. 1987). A letter sent by a physician to the chairperson of the anesthesia department to explain complications a patient suffered during a cesarean delivery is not subject to discovery in an ensuing medical malpractice suit because her letter was written to provide information at a medical staff meeting to review the incident.

Spinks v. Children's Hospital National Medical Center, 124 F.D.R. 9 (D.D.C. 1989). District of Columbia law privileges hospital committee records unless an extraordinary necessity to obtain access to these records is demonstrated. A patient failed to demonstrate an extraordinary need to access the minutes from a morbidity and mortality committee meeting by arguing that she was anesthetized when the injury occurred, that the only witnesses to the event were hospital employees, and that the information was relevant to her suit. In addition, the federal trial court ruled that while the handwritten notes that a physician relied on in making his submission to the committee were not protected from discovery under the statute, a privilege nonetheless applies because disclosure would undermine the effectiveness of hospital committees and be contrary to the public interest.

Jackson v. Scott, C.A. No. 9954-89 (D.C. Ct. App. 1991). The peer review records of a physician, who was sued for malpractice ten years after the investigation, were discoverable although the hospital had entered into a settlement with the physician to remove certain documents from his file.

FLORIDA

Statutory Provisions

Fla. Stat. Ch. 766.101.

The proceedings, investigations, and records of medical staff, peer review, and medical review committees are not subject to discovery or admissible into evidence in any civil action against a health care provider arising out of matters that are the subject of committee evaluation and review. However, material otherwise available from original sources is not immune from discovery or use in civil actions.

Selected Cases

Carter v. Metropolitan Dade County, 253 So.2d 920 (Fla. 1971). Minutes of a hospital teaching session are inadmissible.

Good Samaritan Hospital Ass'n. v. Simon, 370 So.2d 1174 (Fla. 1979). Discovery is allowed where plaintiff physician alleges that the medical review committee acted fraudulently and maliciously in denying him staff privileges.

Dade County Medical Association v. Hlis, 372 So.2d 117 (Fla. 1979). Discovery of ethics committee records in a context different from the civil action against a health care provider is prohibited on public policy grounds.

Segal v. Roberts, 380 So.2d 1049 (Fla. 1979). Section 768.40 of the Florida statute is not applicable where the subject matter of the lawsuit is different from the subject considered by the medical review committee, but discovery of the committee's records is prohibited nevertheless on public policy grounds.

Gadd v. News–Press Publishing Co., 412 So.2d 894 (Fla. Ct. App. 1982). Minutes and documents of a public hospital's utilization review committee are subject to public inspection under the Florida Public Records Act because no specific exemption or confidentiality requirement for such files is provided by statute.

City of Williston v. Roadlander, 425 So.2d 1175 (Fla. Ct. App. 1983). Florida's medical staff committee records confidentiality statute may not be circumvented by claiming that in a public hospital, medical review committee records are public records.

Holly v. Auld, 450 So.2d 217 (Fla. 1984). Physician-applicant for staff privileges was not entitled to discover credential committee records to prove his allegations that he had been defamed. Florida's peer review records confidentiality statute is not limited to malpractice actions but applies as well to defamation actions arising out of matters that are the subject of evaluation and review.

Palm Beach Gardens Community Hospital v. Shaw, 446 So.2d 1090 (Fla. Ct. App. 1984). Monthly reports of a hospital's infectious disease control committee are immune from discovery in a medical malpractice suit because Florida law provides a privilege from discovery for the records of a medical review committee.

Mercy Hospital v. Department of Professional Regulation, Board of Medical Examiners, 467 So.2d 1058 (Fla. Ct. App. 1985). Peer review committee reports and records may be obtained by the state Department of Professional Regulation (DPR) in connection with a disciplinary investigation. Florida's peer review record confidentiality law shields records from discovery only in a civil action, and a DPR investigation is an administrative disciplinary investigation to which the statute does not apply.

Suwannee County Hospital Corp. v. Meeks, 472 So.2d 1305 (Fla. Ct. App. 1985). The proceedings and records of a medical staff committee are not subject to discovery even if no peer review was conducted at a committee meeting; Florida law broadly protects from discovery the records of committees "formed to evaluate and improve the quality of health care rendered."

Davis v. Sarasota County Public Hospital Board, 480 So.2d 203 (Fla. Ct. App. 1985). A public hospital's bills incurred for legal services rendered during peer review proceedings are exempt from discovery.

Burton v. Becker, 516 So.2d 283 (Fla. Ct. App. 1987). A patient suing a physician for medical malpractice may not discover a hospital's peer review records relating to the physician, even when the information is essential to the patient's case.

Ruiz v. Steiner, 599 S.2d 196 (Fla. Ct. App. 1992). An informal meeting of physicians to discuss a pathologist's autopsy report is not a peer review proceeding.

Cruger v. Love, 599 So.2d 111 (Fla. 1992). The peer review confidentiality statute protects any document considered by the committee as part of its decision-making process. In this medical malpractice suit against a physician, the court accordingly concluded that the physician's application for staff privileges was protected from discovery.

GEORGIA

Statutory Provisions

Ga. Code Ann. §§31-7-131 through 31-7-133 and 31-7-143.
Records and proceedings of any panel, committee, or organization, the function of which is to evaluate and improve the quality of health care rendered by health care providers or to reduce morbidity or mortality are not subject to discovery or introduction into evidence against a provider of professional health

care services arising out of matters that are the subject of evaluation and review, except in proceedings alleging violation of the peer review act itself. Review organizations include groups that furnish health care providers with professional liability insurance, thereby extending confidentiality to reviews conducted to evaluate claims against health care providers or to make underwriting decisions concerning health care liability insurance coverage. Peer review organizations also include the Joint Commission on Accreditation of Healthcare Organizations and other national accreditation bodies. However, information, documents, or records otherwise available from original sources are not immune from discovery or use in civil actions simply because they were presented to a committee.

Selected Cases

Hollowell v. Jove, 279 S.E.2d 430 (Ga. 1981). Medical review committee records concerning a physician's care of a particular patient and that physician's care of other patients—and even a listing of the persons who were present at those review meetings—are totally exempt from discovery in Georgia.

Emory Clinic v. Houston, 396 S.E.2d 913 (Ga. 1988). The state peer review statute imposes an absolute bar on the use of all peer records in civil litigation. Prior newspaper reports containing information about a peer review committee's activities do not alter the prohibition on discovery.

Ga. Code Ann §31-7-131, 31-7-133 as amended by H.B. No. 758 (New Laws 1992). Joint Commission on Accreditation of Healthcare Organizations or other national accreditation bodies to definition of peer review organization; stating that confidentiality provisions do not prevent disclosure of records that are used for licensing purposes.

HAWAII

Statutory Provisions

Haw. Rev. Stat. §624-25.5.

Proceedings and records of peer review committees of hospitals are not subject to discovery. However, this prohibition does not apply to the statements made by any person in attendance at a committee meeting who is a party to an action or proceeding, the subject of which was reviewed at such meeting, or to any person who has requested hospital staff privileges. Other exceptions are noted.

IDAHO

Statutory Provisions

Idaho Code §§39-1392 through 39-1392(d).

Written records of interviews, reports, statements, minutes, memoranda, charts, and materials of any hospital medical staff committee, the function of which is to conduct research concerning hospital patient cases or medical questions or problems arising from hospital patient cases, are neither discoverable nor admissible.

This section does not affect or prohibit the use of documents in hospital proceedings, the dissemination of information for medical purposes, or the admissibility of any original patient records. Other exceptions are noted.

Selected Cases

Murphy v. Wood, 667 P.2d 859 (Idaho App. Ct. 1983). The treatment recommendation of a hospital tumor board could not be admitted into evidence by physicians defending against a medical malpractice suit because Idaho law prevents disclosure of medical staff committee proceedings.

ILLINOIS

Statutory Provisions

735 Ill. Comp. Stat. Ann. §§5/8-2101 and 2102.
Information, interviews, reports, statements, memoranda, or other data of patient care audit, medical care evaluation, utilization review, and similar committees of hospitals or medical staffs are strictly confidential and are not admissible. However, the claim of confidentiality cannot be invoked in any hospital proceeding concerning a physician's staff privileges or in a judicial review of such a proceeding to prevent the physician from accessing the data on which the decision was based.

Selected Cases

Matviuw v. Johnson, 388 N.E.2d 795 (Ill. App. Ct. 1979). Plaintiff physician is permitted to discover and use medical staff committee data in a defamation action.

Walker v. Alton Memorial Hospital Association, 414 N.E.2d 850 (Ill. App. Ct. 1980). The hospital was ordered to submit peer review records to a judge for private examination to determine whether the material was inadmissible at trial.

Mennes v. South Chicago Community Hospital, 427 N.E.2d 952 (Ill. App. Ct. 1981). Private judicial examination of peer review committee material relating to the granting of physicians' privileges or reappointment is not necessary because such information is nondiscoverable, regardless of the content of such material.

Jenkins v. Wu, 468 N.E.2d 1162 (Ill. 1984). Constitutionality of state peer review records confidentiality statute reinstated after trial court erroneously declared law invalid. Such records are not discoverable or admissible in medical malpractice actions; exception for physicians defending their staff privileges is rationally related to state's interest in safeguarding the physician's right to due process.

Gleason v. St. Elizabeth Medical Center, 481 N.E.2d 780 (Ill. App. Ct. 1985). Remedial actions taken by a hospital pursuant to peer review of a staff physician are not shielded from discovery. Only the peer review process itself is nondiscoverable.

Richter v. Diamond, 483 N.E.2d 1256 (Ill. 1985). Information concerning whether a physician's hospital staff privileges were restricted as well as the specific restrictions imposed may be discovered from a hospital by a patient suing for malpractice because such information is outside the scope of the state peer review confidentiality law.

Flannery v. Lin, 531 N.E.2d 403 (Ill. Ct. App. 1988). The peer review privilege was applied to protect a "Code Blue Evaluation Report" under the Medical Studies Act. The report was used for internal quality control and was not part of the patient's medical record. It had been prepared by the director of quality management, reviewed by a hospital committee, and its recommendations had been implemented by the hospital's medical officer.

Willing v. St. Joseph Hospital, 531 N.E.2d 824 (Ill. Ct. App. 1988). Records relating to a physician's application for staff privileges and to the granting or modifying of such privileges are not shielded from disclosure in medical malpractice actions under the Medical Studies Act.

Ekstrom v. Temple, 553 N.E.2d 424 (Ill. Ct. App. 1990). A hospital's records relating to infection control were discoverable in a medical malpractice suit against the facility, although documents reflecting investigations and deliberations of committees that monitor infection control were not discoverable under the Medical Studies Act. The hospital failed to provide any evidence regarding the nature and content of the documents, and the court refused to apply the privilege to all the materials based on the claim that some of the materials might be privileged.

INDIANA

Statutory Provisions

Ind. Code Ann. §§34-4-12.6-1 and 34-4-12.6-2.
Records of the determinations of or communications to a peer review committee are not subject to discovery or admissible into evidence without a prior waiver executed by the committee. Information otherwise discoverable or admissible from original sources is not immune from discovery or use simply because it was presented during committee meetings. In addition, any professional health care provider who is under investigation has the right to see any records pertaining to his or her personal practice. Other exceptions noted.

Selected Cases

Parkview Memorial Hospital v. Pepple, 483 N.E.2d 469 (Ind. Ct. App. 1985). Indiana's peer review confidentiality law applies not only to medical malpractice cases but to civil actions brought by physicians challenging private hospitals' decisions concerning staff privileges as well. A physician seeking judicial review of a private hospital's adverse recommendation concerning recredentialing was, therefore, prohibited from introducing evidence relating to the hospital's peer review committee proceedings.

Terre Haute Regional Hospital, Inc. v. Basden, 524 N.E.2d 1306 (Ind. Ct. App. 1988). Although peer review committee members are immune from liability only if they act in good faith, peer review information that is protected from disclosure does not become subject to disclosure due to lack of good faith on the part of the committee members.

Ray v. St. John's Health Care Corp., 582 N.E. 2d 464 (Ind. Ct. App. 1991). A trial court should have conducted an in-camera review of documents sought by physicians in a suit against a hospital to determine whether the peer review privilege applied. The hospital's labels for these documents and the chief executive officer's statement that they were privileged were not decisive.

IOWA

Statutory Provisions

Iowa Code Ann. §147.135.
Peer review records are privileged and confidential, are not subject to discovery, subpoena, or other means of legal compulsion, and are not admissible in evidence in judicial or administrative proceedings except when a licensee's competence or disciplinary status is at issue. A person shall not be liable as a result of filing a report with or providing information to a peer review committee or for disclosure of privileged matter to a peer review committee. A person present at a peer review committee meeting shall not be permitted to testify as to the findings or opinions of the committee in any judicial or administrative proceeding.

Selected Cases

Boger v. Lee, No. 49568 (D. Iowa June 16, 1982). Information produced by the activities of a professional standards review organization (PSRO) or a hospital performing the function of a PSRO is not subject to subpoena or discovery in a civil action except to the extent that the hospital contemplates using the information at trial.

Hutchison v. Smith Laboratories, Inc., 392 N.W.2d 139 (Iowa 1986). The records of a medical staff peer review committee and evaluation reports of a drug injection procedure performed on a patient are discoverable and not entitled to privilege based on common law or public policy.

KANSAS

Statutory Provisions

Kan. Stat. Ann. §65-4915.
Proceedings and records of peer review committees and officers are privileged and are not discoverable or admissible in evidence in any judicial or administrative proceeding. This privilege does not apply to proceedings in which a health care provider contests the denial or status of staff privileges or authorization to practice.

Selected Cases

Wesley Medical Center v. Clark, 669 P.2d 209 (Kan. 1983). The records of medical peer review committee proceedings may be discovered in a medical malpractice action because no statutory privilege for such records exists in the

Kansas evidence code. However, a court may limit disclosure if it determines that a hospital's interest in confidentiality outweighs the need for the evidence.

Fretz v. Keltner, 109 F.R.D. 303 (D. Kan. 1986). The Joint Commission functions as a peer review committee, and therefore, its accreditation documents are not discoverable.

Porter v. Snyder, 115 F.R.D. 77 (D. Kan. 1987). Kansas peer review legislation protecting the reports of executive or review committees does not protect hospital incident reports from discovery in a patient's malpractice suit. Incident reports are not reports made by a review committee but rather are contemporaneous statements of fact relating to incidents reviewed by a committee.

Jiricko v. Coffeyville Memorial Hospital Medical Center, 700 F. Supp. 1559 (D. Kan. 1988). Peer review activities in Kansas are not immune from scrutiny under federal antitrust law because the state does not actively supervise peer review decisions. When both state and federal antitrust claims are made, the question of privilege is controlled by federal law rather than the state peer review statute. Peer review privilege will not be recognized when there is a claim that the peer review process was abused as part of the antitrust conspiracy because to deny discovery in such circumstances would effectively prevent the physician from suing.

Hill v. Sandu, No. 89–1338–C (D. Kan. Jan. 24, 1990). A patient suing a physician for medical malpractice is entitled to discover documents submitted to a peer review committee relating to the physician's award of staff privileges. The documents concerned the hospital's awarding of staff privileges to the physician and were not privileged simply because the committee had referred to them when reviewing the physician.

Herbstreith v. Baker, 815 P.2d 102 (Kan. 1991). Peer review records were not admissible in a medical malpractice case against a physician in which there were allegations relating to the physician's qualifications.

KENTUCKY

Statutory Provisions

Ky. Rev. Stat. §311.377.

The proceedings, records, opinions, conclusions, and recommendations of any committee, board, commission, PSRO, or other entity, the purpose of which is to review and evaluate the credentials or competency of professional acts or conduct of other health care personnel, are confidential and privileged; they are not subject to discovery, subpoena, or introduction into evidence in any civil action, court, or administrative proceeding. This statute does not protect materials that are independently discoverable or admissible, nor does it restrict or prevent the presentation of records and other materials in any statutory or administrative proceeding relating to the functions of any committee or other review body. Other exceptions are noted.

Selected Cases

Sweasy v. King's Daughters Memorial Hospital, 771 S.W.2d 812 (Ky. 1989). The supreme court in this state has ruled that peer review records created by hospital peer review committees are only confidential in suits against peer review entities and can be discovered in medical malpractice suits.

LOUISIANA

Statutory Provisions

La. Rev. Stat. §§44:7 and 13:3715.3.
The records and proceedings of public and private hospital committees, medical organization committees, or extended care facilities are not public records and are not available for court subpoena. The peer review committee records of group medical practices of more than 20 physicians, freestanding surgical centers, and HMOs are confidential and are not available for discovery in litigation except for proceedings relating to a physician's staff privileges. In such proceedings, only the physician or other health care professional who is the object of an adverse decision with respect to staff privileges may obtain the records.

A medical staff member whose privileges are adversely affected by a decision of any hospital committee, medical organization committee, or extended care facility committee may obtain the records forming the basis of the decision, notwithstanding the confidentiality provisions of §44:7.

Selected Cases

Kadan v. City of New Orleans, 596 So.2d 1306 (La. 1992). Hospital peer review records are confidential under state law and not subject to subpoena or discovery in court cases.

MAINE

Statutory Provisions

Me. Rev. Stat. tit. 32, §§3296 and 92-A.
All proceedings and records of proceedings of mandatory medical staff review committees and hospital review committees are exempt from discovery. All records of proceedings concerning quality assurance activities of any emergency medical service quality assurance committee are exempt from discovery.

MARYLAND

Statutory Provisions

Md. Code Ann. [Health Occ.] §14-501.
The proceedings, records, and files of a medical review committee are neither discoverable nor admissible into evidence in any civil action arising out of matters that are the subject of committee evaluation and review. A medical review committee is a committee of the medical staff or other committee, including any risk management, credentialing, or utilization review committee, of a hospital if the governing board forms and approves the committee or approves the written bylaws under which the committee operates.

Selected Cases

Unnamed Physician v. Commission on Medical Discipline, 400 A.2d 396 (Md. 1979). The proceedings, records, and other documents of medical staff committees are discoverable in physician disciplinary proceedings but not in civil suits.

Kappas v. Chestnut Lodge, 709 F.2d 878 (4th Cir. 1983), *cert. denied*, 104 S. Ct. 164 (1983). Transcripts of a psychiatric hospital's medical staff conferences that evaluated patient care and treatment were not admissible because they qualified as reports of "medical review committee" proceedings.

Baltimore Sun v. University of Maryland Medical Center, 584 A.2d 683 (Md. 1991). Peer review confidentiality legislation does not prevent the press from accessing records that were introduced as evidence in a physician's staff privileges suit against the hospital.

MASSACHUSETTS

Statutory Provisions

Mass. Ann. Laws ch. 11, §§204(a) and 205(b).

Records necessary to comply with risk management and quality assurance programs that are necessary to the work product of medical peer review committees, including incident reports required to be furnished to the board of medicine, are proceedings, reports, or records of medical peer review committees. Such records are confidential and are not subject to disclosure unless they have been disclosed in an adjudicatory proceeding of the board of medicine. No person shall be prevented from testifying as to matters known by such person independent of risk management and quality assurance programs. Reports and records of a medical peer review committee are confidential and are not discoverable or admissible in any judicial or administrative proceeding except proceedings by the boards of registration in medicine, social work, or psychology.

Selected Cases

Commonwealth v. Choate-Symmes Health Services, Inc., 545 N.E.2d 1167 (Mass. 1989). The Massachusetts Board of Registration in Medicine does not have a right of access to peer review committee records when it is investigating a complaint concerning a physician's conduct. State legislation only grants the board access to these documents within its administrative proceedings.

MICHIGAN

Statutory Provisions

Mich. Comp. Laws §§333.20175 and 333.21515.

The records, data, and knowledge collected for or by individuals or committees assigned a professional review function in a health facility or agency are confidential, shall be used only for the purposes that are legislatively authorized, are not public records, and are not subject to court subpoena.

Selected Cases

Marchand v. Henry Ford Hospital, 247 N.W.2d 280 (Mich. 1976). Information collected by individuals other than those sitting on a professional practices review committee is discoverable.

Monty v. Warren Hospital Corp., 366 N.W.2d 198 (Mich. 1985). Hospital personnel files of staff physicians must be produced for a private, in-camera court inspection when sought for discovery in a malpractice action. The court must determine whether the information therein is privileged under the state peer review record confidentiality law or whether the information may be discovered.

In re Petition of Attorney General, 369 N.W.2d 826 (Mich. 1985). A hospital cannot be required to disclose peer review committee records, data, and knowledge collected during a disciplinary investigation, notwithstanding that the information is sought in connection with an investigation by the state department of licensing and regulation.

MINNESOTA

Statutory Provisions

Minn. Stat. §§145.61-145.65.

Data and information of quality assurance, mortality and morbidity, cost control, and similar committees are not subject to subpoena or discovery. The proceedings and records of these committees are not subject to discovery or introduction into evidence in any civil action against a health care professional arising out of matters that are the subject of evaluation and review. However, documents or records otherwise available from original sources are not immune simply because they were presented during the proceedings of a review organization. This statute does not apply to committees that function to grant or deny staff privileges.

Selected Cases

Kalish v. Mt. Sinai Hospital, 270 N.W.2d 783 (Minn. 1978). Guidelines of a hospital medical staff committee are discoverable but not admissible.

In re Proposed Suspension or Non-Renewal of Nursing Home Licenses of Parkway Manor Healthcare Center and Innsbruck Healthcare Center, 448 N.W.2d 116 (Minn. Ct. App. 1989). The court rejected claims that a nursing center's quality assurance records were privileged, finding that the quality assurance program was not a review organization within the meaning of the statute.

MISSISSIPPI

Statutory Provisions

Miss. Code Ann. §41-63-9.

The proceedings and records of medical review committees are not subject to discovery or introduction into evidence in any civil action against a health care provider arising out of matters that are the subject of evaluation and review.

However, information, documents, and records that are otherwise discoverable from original sources are not immune from discovery merely because they were presented to a committee. This statute does not apply to legal actions brought by a committee to restrict or revoke a physician's license or privileges or in any action brought against a committee or its members for actions alleged to be malicious.

MISSOURI

Statutory Provisions

Mo. Ann. Stat. §537.035.

The proceedings, findings, deliberations, reports, and minutes of peer review committees are not discoverable or admissible in any judicial or administrative action for failure to provide appropriate care. No person at any peer review committee proceeding may be permitted or required to disclose any information obtained. However, information otherwise discoverable from original sources is not immune from discovery merely because it was presented to a committee. This statute does not apply to legal actions brought by a committee to deny, restrict, or revoke a physician's privileges or license to practice. Further, the state health care licensing board may obtain confidential information from peer review committees within its jurisdiction.

Selected Cases

State ex rel. Faith Hospital v. Enright, 706 S.W.2d 852 (Mo. 1986). Even though a credentials committee is a peer review committee, its findings and deliberations are not exempt from discovery unless they specifically concern the health care provided to a patient.

MONTANA

Statutory Provisions

Mont. Code Ann. §§50-16-201, 50-16-203 through 50-16-205.

Data (written reports, notes, and records) of tissue committees and committees that function to assist in the training, supervision, and discipline of health care professionals are confidential and are not admissible in evidence in any judicial proceeding. This statute does not affect the admissibility of records dealing with a patient's hospital care and treatment.

Sistok v. Kalispell Regional Hospital, 823 P.2d 251 (Mont. 1991). Records of a medical executive committee are absolutely privileged and are not discoverable in a medical malpractice suit by a patient alleging that the hospital negligently allowed him to perform surgery knowing he had a history of alcoholism.

NEBRASKA

Statutory Provisions

Neb. Rev. Stat. §71-2046 through 71-2048.

The proceedings, records, minutes, reports, and communications of medical staff committees and utilization review committees are not subject to discovery except upon court order after a showing of good cause arising from extraordinary circumstances and waiver by the patient. This statute does not preclude or affect discovery or production of evidence relating to the hospitalization or treatment of any patient in the ordinary course of hospitalization of such patient.

Selected Cases

Oviatt v. Archbishop Bergan Mercy Hospital, 214 N.W.2d 490 (Neb. 1974). The proceedings of a hospital medical staff committee are privileged in the absence of a showing of good cause arising from extraordinary circumstances.

NEVADA

Statutory Provisions

Nev. Rev. Stat. Ann. §49.265.

The proceedings and records of medical review committees and organized medical staff committees responsible for evaluating and improving the quality of care rendered in hospitals are not subject to discovery. However, this statute does not apply to any statement made by an applicant for hospital staff privileges; nor does it apply to any statement made by a person in attendance at a committee meeting who is a party to an action or proceeding, the subject of which is reviewed at such meeting. Other exceptions noted.

NEW HAMPSHIRE

Statutory Provisions

N.H. Rev. Stat. Ann. §329.29.

All proceedings, records, findings, and deliberations of medical review committees are confidential and privileged and are not to be used, available for use, or subject to process in any other proceeding.

Selected Cases

In re K., 561 A.2d 1063 (N.H. 1989). A report prepared by a nurse epidemiologist and submitted to a hospital's infection control committee relating to how a maternity patient contracted herpes is privileged under New Hampshire law. The statutory privilege that applies to QA activities is not confined to a single committee.

NEW JERSEY

Statutory Provisions

N.J. Stat. §2A:84A-22.8.

Information and data secured by utilization review committees may not be revealed or disclosed in any manner or in any circumstances except to (1) a patient's attending physician, (2) the chief administrative officer of a hospital that such committees serve, (3) the medical executive committee of a hospital, (4) representatives of governmental agencies in the performance of their duties, or (5) insurance companies under certain circumstances.

Selected Cases

Myers v. St. Francis Hospital, 220 A.2d 693 (N.J. Super. Ct. App. Div. 1966). Discovery rules are to be construed liberally in the absence of any indication therein to the contrary. (This case was decided prior to the enactment of §2A:84A-22.8.)

Gureghian v. Hackensack Hospital, 262 A.2d 440 (N.J. Super. Ct. Law Div. 1970). Records of a perinatal mortality committee are discoverable. (This case was decided prior to the enactment of §2A:84A-22.8.)

Young v. King, 344 A.2d 792 (N.J. Super. Ct. Law Div. 1975). Section 2A:84A-22.8 applies to information and data of utilization committees but not to information and data of medical records committees, tissue committees, or infection control committees.

Garrow v. Elizabeth General Hospital & Dispensary, 401 A.2d 533 (N.J. 1979). A physician is entitled to discover data used by a hospital medical staff in its decision to reject his application for staff privileges.

Bundy v. Sinopoli, 580 A.2d 1101 (N.J. Super. Ct. 1990). Opinions, criticisms, and evaluations contained in peer review committee files are protected from discovery in medical malpractice suit.

NEW MEXICO

Statutory Provisions

N.M. Stat. Ann. §§41-9-2 and 41-9-5.

Data and information of cost control, quality assurance, mortality and morbidity, and similar committees are confidential and not subject to discovery. However, information, documents, and records otherwise available from original sources are not immune from discovery or use in any civil action merely because they were presented during the proceedings of a review organization. Material is not protected if it is sought to be used in a judicial appeal from an action of a review organization.

Selected Cases

University Heights Hospital, Inc. v. Ashby, No. 14284 (N.M. June 16, 1982). Constitutionality of state peer review act reinstated after a trial court erroneously invalidated the confidentiality provisions of the act.

Southwest Community Health Services v. Smith, 755 P.2d 40 (N.M.1988). The court upheld the constitutionality of the state peer review statute but ruled that when a plaintiff is able to demonstrate that privileged information is critical to the case, the court may, in its discretion, declare such evidence admissible.

NEW YORK

Statutory Provisions

N.Y. Educ. Law §6527(3).

Proceedings and records of utilization review, quality control, and similar committees are not subject to disclosure. This exemption from disclosure does not apply to statements made by any person in attendance at a committee meeting who is a party to an action or proceeding, the subject of which was reviewed at the meeting. Other exceptions are noted.

Selected Cases

Judd v. Park Avenue Hospital, 235 N.Y.S.2d 843 (Monroe County Sup. Ct. 1962). Hospital medical staff committee discussions are considered hearsay and, therefore, not subject to discovery. (This case was decided prior to the enactment of §6527.)

Salmonsen v. Brown, 309 N.Y.S.2d 535 (Onondaga County Sup. Ct. 1970). The hospital's failure to apply for a protective order constitutes a waiver of immunity from discovery. (This case was decided prior to the enactment of §6527.)

Gourdine v. Phelps Memorial Hospital, 336 N.Y.S.2d 316 (App. Div. 1972). The court will not compel disclosure of documents of medical staff meetings where it is apparent that no such documents exist.

Pinder v. Parke Davis & Co., 337 N.Y.S.2d 452 (Schoharie County Sup. Ct. 1972). Section 6527 does not protect statements of a person in attendance at a medical staff committee meeting who is a party to an action or proceeding, the subject of which was reviewed at such meeting.

Lang v. Abbott Laboratories, 398 N.Y.S.2d 577 (App. Div. 1977). Discovery of hospital records concerning quality of intravenous fluid is not barred by §6527.

Lenard v. New York University Medical Center, 442 N.Y.S.2d 30 (App. Div. 1982). Statements by members of a hospital's medical review committee are not discoverable if the hospital, by itself, is a party to a medical malpractice suit but would be discoverable if a member of the committee were a party to the lawsuit.

DePaolo v. Wisoff, 461 N.Y.S.2d 893 (App. Div. 1983). Minutes of hospital staff meetings are not discoverable in a malpractice action, but statements made by individual parties to the suit and contained in the minutes may be obtained after the court's private inspection of the minutes and deletion of privileged material.

Daly v. Genovese, 466 N.Y.S.2d 428 (App. Div. 1983). Allegedly slanderous statements made in peer review proceedings are not discoverable in a defamation action. Only statements concerning the subject matter of peer review proceedings may be discovered.

Palmer v. City of Rome, 466 N.Y.S.2d 238 (App. Div. 1983). Pathology reports prepared for use in evaluating the clinical performance of a physician are immune from discovery in a medical malpractice action even though the reviewing physicians did not constitute a "committee" as defined by New York's medical review confidentiality statute.

Byork v. Carmer, 487 N.Y.S.2d 226 (App. Div. 1985). Hospital review committee confidentiality statute does not protect from discovery in a malpractice suit a hospital's knowledge of alleged prior negligent acts of staff physician because such knowledge may be acquired from sources who did not participate in privileged review committee meetings.

Lilly v. Turecki, 492 N.Y.S.2d 286 (App. Div. 1985). New York's peer review confidentiality law satisfies due process requirements because it is a reasonable means for promoting and improving the quality of medical care; hospital review committee documents sought by patient in malpractice suit must be submitted to malpractice panel's presiding justice for determination of discoverability.

Parker v. St. Clare's Hospital, 553 N.Y.S.2d 533 (N.Y. App. Div. 1990). In a suit against a hospital charging it with negligent physician credentialing, documents pertaining to the physician's initial application for privileges and renewal applications were protected from discovery.

St. Elizabeth's Hospital v. State Board of Professional Medical Conduct, 579 N.Y.S.2d 457 (N.Y. App. Div. 1992). A medical conduct review board could subpoena a hospital's quality assurance committee records to investigate professional misconduct.

NORTH CAROLINA

Statutory Provisions

N.C. Gen. Stat. §§131E-76 and §§131E-95.

The records, proceedings, and materials considered or produced by a committee that evaluates the quality, cost, or necessity of hospitalization or health care services are not discoverable or admissible in a civil action against a provider of professional health services where the action arises out of matters that are the subject of evaluation and review by the committee and are not public records.

Selected Cases

Shelton v. Morehead Memorial Hospital, 322 S.E.2d 499 (N.C. Ct. App. 1985). The state's peer review confidentiality law prevents discovery of information from a hospital's former chief executive officer who participated in review committee proceedings as well as from the review committee itself. The minutes of a hospital's board of trustees may be discovered, however, because the board is not charged with peer review functions.

NORTH DAKOTA

Statutory Provisions

N.D. Cent. Code §23-01-02.1.

Any information, data, reports, or records made available to a mandatory hospital committee or internal quality assurance review committee are confidential and can only be used for the proper functions of the committees. Information, documents, or records that are otherwise discoverable will not be confidential merely because they were presented at a review committee hearing, nor can witnesses be prevented from testifying in a suit merely because they testified before the committee.

OHIO

Statutory Provisions

Ohio Rev. Code Ann. §2305.24.

Proceedings and records of tissue, utilization review, peer review, and similar committees are confidential and are not subject to discovery or introduction into evidence in any civil action arising out of matters that are the subject of evaluation and review. However, information, documents, or records otherwise available from original sources are not immune from discovery or use merely because they were presented during committee meetings.

Selected Cases

Samuelson v. Susen, 576 F.2d 546 (3d Cir. 1978). The Ohio statute protecting committee records does not deprive a litigant of Fifth and Fourteenth Amendment due process rights.

Young v. Gersten, 381 N.E.2d 353 (Franklin County C.P. 1978). The Ohio statute protecting committee records does not violate the Ohio Constitution.

Rees v. Doctor's Hospital, No. CA-5226 (Ohio App., Stark County Feb. 6, 1980). Hospital incident reports are discoverable in a civil action against a hospital.

Gates v. Brewer, 442 N.E.2d 72 (Ohio App. 1981). When an individual attempts to prevent the discovery of information by asserting the privilege provided by the Ohio statute that prohibits the discovery of review committees' records, it is incumbent on the trial court to hold an in-camera inspection of the information, documents, and records in question to ensure that all the material sought to be discovered is, in fact, protected under the statute.

Fostoria Daily Review Co. v. Fostoria Hospital Association, 541 N.E.2d 587 (Ohio 1989). A public hospital's joint advisory and quality assurance committee was not covered by Ohio legislation that protects the records of hospital review committees from discovery in malpractice suits. The committee did not perform quality assurance reviews itself but instead received reports from a subsidiary quality assurance committee.

Lemasters v. Christ Hospital, 791 F.Supp. 188 (S.D. Ohio 1991). A physician was entitled to discover peer review information in her suit claiming sex discrimination against a hospital in its decision to suspend her privileges. The physician's right to sue for discrimination and her need for information to prove her allegations outweighed the hospital's claim to confidentiality.

OKLAHOMA

Statutory Provisions

Okla. Stat. Ann. tit. 63, §1-1709.

All information, interviews, reports, statements, memoranda, findings, and conclusions of committees formed for the purpose of advancing medical research or medical education in the interest of reducing morbidity and mortality are not to be used, offered, or received in evidence in any legal proceeding.

Selected Cases

City of Edmond v. Parr, 587 P.2d 56 (Okla. 1978). Records kept by a hospital infectious disease control committee and records pertaining to an investigation concerning infection in the hospital or among patients and employees are inadmissible in a malpractice action.

OREGON

Statutory Provisions

Or. Rev. Stat. §41.675.

All data of tissue, utilization review, and similar committees are confidential and are not admissible in evidence in any judicial proceeding, except where a health care practitioner contests the denial, restriction, or termination of clinical privileges. This statute, however, does not affect the admissibility in evidence of records dealing with a patient's hospital care and treatment.

Selected Cases

Straube v. Larson, 600 P.2d 371 (Or. 1979). Section 41.675 is applicable to medical staff disciplinary committees as well as to hospital tissue committees.

PENNSYLVANIA

Statutory Provisions

Pa. Stat. Ann. tit. 63, §§425.2 and 425.4.

The proceedings and records of peer review, utilization review, medical audit, claims review, and similar committees are not subject to discovery or introduction into evidence in any civil action against a professional health care provider arising out of matters that are the subject of evaluation and review. However, information, documents, or records otherwise available from original sources are not immune simply because they were presented during committee proceedings.

Selected Cases

Robinson v. Magovern, 83 F.R.D. 79 (W.D. Pa. 1979). Pursuant to Rule 501 of the Federal Rules of Evidence, records of hospital medical staff credentials and executive committees are discoverable in federal antitrust action and in a pendent state claim, despite §425.4.

Hankinson v. Threshold, Inc., No. 1482 of 1992 (Pa. Ct. of Common Pleas, Westmoreland County, Aug. 19, 1992). The records of a committee that investigated the murder of one patient by another patient are not protected by peer review privilege. The committee in this case was appointed in response to the particular incident and was not charged with evaluating and improving care.

Swarthmore Radiation Oncology Inc. v. Lapes, No. 92-3055 (E.D. Pa. Nov. 15, 1993). A hospital's staff privilege files are discoverable in a suit alleging antitrust violation by a group of physicians and hospitals in an attempt to force a radiation center for cancer out of business.

RHODE ISLAND

Statutory Provisions

R.I. Gen. Laws §§5-37.3-7 and 23-17-25.
Proceedings and records of medical peer review committees are not subject to discovery or introduction into evidence. However, information otherwise discoverable or admissible from original sources is not immune simply because it was presented during committee proceedings. This statute does not prohibit discovery in legal actions brought by a medical review committee to restrict or revoke a physician's license or staff privileges or in legal actions brought by aggrieved physicians. Other exceptions are noted.

Selected Cases

Cofone v. Westerly Hospital, 504 A.2d 998 (R.I. 1986). A medical staff infection control committee is a "peer review board," as defined by the state peer review confidentiality law, and its proceedings, therefore, are not subject to discovery.

Moretti v. Lowe, 592 A.2d 855 (R.I. 1991). Peer review legislation does not protect from discovery information that was otherwise available from original sources, even if the information was presented at peer review committee meetings. Accordingly, the court ruled that the hospital should identify all persons who have knowledge of the alleged incident of malpractice regardless of whether the person sits on the peer review committee or has presented evidence to the committee.

SOUTH CAROLINA

Statutory Provisions

S.C. Code §§40-71-10 and 40-71-20.
All proceedings and all data and information acquired by committees formed to maintain professional standards are not subject to discovery, subpoena, or introduction into evidence except on appeal from a committee's action. Also, information, documents, and records that are otherwise available from original sources are not immune from discovery or use simply because they were presented before a committee.

Selected Cases

McGee v. Bruce Hospital System, No. 23968 (S.C. Dec. 13, 1993). The state peer review privilege covers information obtained by the medical staff review committee with respect to applications for staff privileges and training documents. However, the same material that is not discoverable from the hospital committee can be discovered if it is available from other sources.

SOUTH DAKOTA

Statutory Provisions

S.D. Codified Laws Ann. 36-4-26.1.

The proceedings, records, reports, statements, minutes, or other data of committees, the function of which is to review the quality, type, or necessity of care rendered by a health care provider or to evaluate the competence, character, experience, and performance of a physician, are not subject to disclosure or introduction into evidence. However, the prohibition relating to discovery of evidence does not apply in situations in which a physician seeks access to information on which a decision regarding his or her staff privileges was based.

TENNESSEE

Statutory Provisions

Tenn. Code Ann. §63-6-219.

All information, interviews, statements, or other data furnished to any medical review committee are confidential and are not available for subpoena or discovery. However, material that is otherwise available from original sources is not protected merely because it was presented before a committee. Other exceptions to the general rule of nondiscoverability are noted.

Selected Cases

Patton v. Mishra, No. 83-24-II (Tenn. Ct. App. Mar. 9, 1984). Suspension or other punitive action taken by a hospital against a medical staff member is protected from discovery by the peer review confidentiality statute.

TEXAS

Statutory Provisions

Tex. Rev. Civ. Stat. Ann. art. 4495(b).

All proceedings and records of a medical peer review committee are confidential and all communications made to a medical peer review committee are privileged. However, if a judge makes a preliminary finding that such proceedings, records, or communications are relevant to an anticompetitive action or a civil rights proceeding brought under Chapter 42, U.S.C.A. 1983, then such proceedings, records, and communications are not confidential to the extent they are deemed relevant.

Selected Cases

Karp v. Cooley, 493 F.2d 408 (5th Cir. 1974). Records of medical school investigating committees are protected by Article 4447d.

Texarkana Memorial Hospital v. Jones, 551 S.W.2d 33 (Tex. 1977). Minutes of medical staff meetings are protected by Article 4447d from discovery in a medical malpractice action.

Hood v. Phillips, 554 S.W.2d 160 (Tex. 1977). A physician's private records are not protected by Article 4447d.

Jordan v. Court of Appeals, 701 S.W.2d 644 (Tex. 1985). The state peer review privilege protects from discovery documents prepared by or at the direction of a hospital committee for committee purposes. The deliberations of a hospital committee, minutes of committee meetings, correspondence between committee members relating to the deliberation process, and any final committee products, such as recommendations, are also not discoverable. However, documents that are gratuitously submitted to a committee or that have been created without committee impetus and purpose are not protected by the privilege and may be discovered.

Santa Rosa Medical Center v. Spears, 709 S.W.2d 720 (Tex. Ct. App. 1986). The discovery privilege is waived only by voluntary disclosure or consent to a disclosure, not by an improper disclosure where the hospital did not have an opportunity to claim the privilege. The identity of committee members, however, is not privileged under the statute.

Northeast Community Hospital v. Gregg, 815 S.W.2d 320 (Tex. Ct. App. 1991). A trial court abused its discretion by ordering production of peer review records specifically protected from discovery by statute without first inspecting the documents in camera.

Manthe v. VanBolden, 133 F.R.D. 497 (N.D. Tex. 1991). In a medical malpractice suit, a hospital's peer review records were privileged and not subject to discovery.

UTAH

Statutory Provisions

Utah Code Ann. §§26-25-1 and 26-25-3.

All information, interviews, reports, statements, memoranda, and other data of committees, the function of which is to reduce morbidity or mortality or to evaluate and improve the quality of hospital and medical care, are privileged and are not to be used or received into evidence in any legal proceeding.

VERMONT

Statutory Provisions

Vt. Stat. Ann. tit. 26, §§1441, 1443.

The proceedings, reports, and records of committees formed to evaluate and improve the quality of health care rendered by providers of health care services or to determine whether services were professionally indicated and performed or whether their cost was reasonable are neither discoverable nor admissible in any civil action against a health care provider arising out of matters that are the subject of evaluation and review. However, information, reports, or documents otherwise available from original sources are not immune from discovery or use in civil actions simply because they were presented before a committee.

Selected Cases

Wheeler v. Central Vermont Medical Center, 582 A.2d 165 (Vt. 1989). In a patient's negligent credentialing suit against a hospital, the patient did not introduce any impermissible evidence from peer review records, and therefore, the hospital was not entitled to present evidence from those records in its defense.

VIRGINIA

Statutory Provisions

Va. Code Ann. §§8.01-581.16 and 8.01-581.17.

The proceedings, records, minutes, reports, and oral and written communications of cost control, utilization review, quality control, peer review, and similar committees are privileged and are not discoverable except upon court order after a showing of good cause arising from extraordinary circumstances. This statute does not immunize hospital records kept with respect to any patient in the ordinary course of the business of operating a hospital.

WASHINGTON

Statutory Provisions

Wash. Rev. Code Ann. §4.24.250.

The proceedings, reports, and written records of committees formed to evaluate the competence and qualifications of members of the health care profession are not subject to subpoena or discovery in any civil action except actions arising out of a committee's recommendations.

Selected Cases

Coburn v. Seda, 677 P.2d 173 (Wash. 1984). The proceedings, reports, and written records of "regularly constituted" hospital quality review committees are immune from discovery in medical malpractice suits.

Anderson v. Breda, 700 P.2d 737 (Wash. 1985). Information concerning the suspension, termination, or restriction of a staff physician's hospital privileges is not privileged under the state peer review confidentiality law when discovered independently from physician named in malpractice action.

WEST VIRGINIA

Statutory Provisions

W. Va. Code §30-3C-3.
The proceedings and records of peer review, utilization review, medical audit, claims review, and similar committees are privileged and are not subject to subpoena, discovery, or introduction into evidence in any civil action arising out of matters that are the subject of evaluation and review. However, documents, information, and records that are otherwise available from original sources are not protected simply because they were presented during committee proceedings. Further, material is available in civil actions to individuals whose activities are under committee scrutiny. Other exceptions are noted.

Selected Cases

State ex. rel. Shroades v. Henry, 421 S.E.2d 264 (W.Va. 1992). The peer review privilege does not preclude discovery of documents created for or by a peer review committee if the documents are otherwise available from other sources.

Young v. Saldanha, No. 21274 (W. Va. April 23, 1993). Under West Virginia law, a physician subject to peer review must formally waive the confidentiality privilege that protects the records of his review. In this case, the physician's submission of peer review information about himself in another civil suit did not qualify as a valid waiver.

WISCONSIN

Statutory Provisions

Wis. Stat. Ann. §146.38.
Records of organizations formed to review and evaluate the services of health care providers may not be used in civil actions against health care providers or facilities. However, information, documents, and records are not to be construed as immune from discovery or use in civil actions merely because they were presented to a committee. Information can be released for medical and other specified purposes as long as the names of patients are withheld.

Selected Cases

Davison v. St. Paul Fire & Marine Insurance Co., 248 N.W.2d 433 (Wis. 1977). There is no statutory or common law immunity from discovery for medical staff committee records. (This case was decided prior to the enactment of §146.38.)

Shibilski v. St. Joseph's Hospital of Marshfield, Inc., 266 N.W.2d 264 (Wis. 1978). Inadmissibility of medical staff committee records is not a bar to their discovery. (This case was decided prior to the enactment of §146.38.)

Jacobs v. Gallagher, No. F3-1471 (Wis. Cir. Ct.–Branch 1, La Crosse County Sept. 16, 1983). The Wisconsin statute that bars discoverability and admissibility of medical staff peer review records is constitutional.

State ex rel. Good Samaritan Medical Center–Deaconess Hospital Campus v. Maroney, 365 N.W.2d 887 (Wis. Ct. App. 1985). Wisconsin hospital records confidentiality statute construed as applying only to a "review or evaluation of the services of a health care provider;" credentials committee records are subject to discovery.

Mallow v. Angove, 434 N.W.2d 839 (Wis. Ct. App. 1988). An amendment to the peer review statute extending statutory immunity to good faith acts by hospital governing bodies does not bring the activities of these bodies within the confidentiality provisions of the statute. Therefore, a patient was entitled to discover information relating to a hospital's governing board's decision to suspend a physician's staff privileges.

WYOMING

Statutory Provisions

Wyo. Stat. §§35-2-601 and 35-2-602.

All reports, findings, proceedings, and data of hospital medical staff committees that are responsible for the supervision, discipline, admission privileges, or control of staff members, or that evaluate and report on patient care and treatment, research, reducing mortality, prevention and treatment of diseases, illnesses and injuries, and utilization review are confidential and privileged.

FEDERAL LAW

Rules

Rule 501, Federal Rules of Evidence, 28 U.S.C. Federal common law is controlling with respect to discovery questions except where state law supplies the rule of decision, in which case state laws governing privilege are controlling.

Selected Cases

Bredice v. Doctors' Hospital, Inc., 50 F.R.D. 249 (D.D.C. 1970). Minutes of a hospital medical staff committee are not subject to discovery without a showing of exceptional necessity.

Gillman v. United States, 53 F.R.D. 316 (S.D.N.Y. 1971). Minutes and reports of a committee inquiring into hospital procedures and behavior of hospital personnel are not discoverable in an action under Federal Tort Claims Act.

Robinson v. Magovern, 83 F.R.D. 79 (W.D. Pa. 1979). Under Rule 501 of the Federal Rules of Evidence, hospital medical staff committee records are discoverable even though privileged under a state statute.

Schafer v. Parkview Memorial Hospital, 593 F. Supp. 61 (N.D. Ind. 1984). Minutes of a hospital psychiatric review committee are discoverable in a suit based on the federal Age Discrimination in Employment Act because the need for discovery outweighs the reasons underlying the privilege provided by the state peer review record confidentiality statute.

Mewborn v. Heckler, 101 F.R.D. 691 (D.D.C. 1984). In an action under the Federal Tort Claims Act, the minutes, reports, or other documents of a peer review committee may not be discovered absent a showing of extraordinary necessity, especially when the raw factual data that is sought can be obtained from other hospital reports and records.

Whitman v. United States, 108 F.R.D. 5 (D.N.H. 1985). Federal law recognizes a privilege protecting hospital peer review records from discovery, but that privilege can be voluntarily waived. Therefore, in an action under the Federal Tort Claims Act, the records of a peer review committee hearing were discoverable because a physician disclosed in a deposition the identity of persons at the hearing and a specialist's statement that the surgery under review was performed improperly. The records were not protected by the attorney's work product rule because the material was not generated in preparation for litigation.

Index _____

Note: Numbers indicate chapter and question numbers not page numbers (e.g., 1:3
    indicates Chapter 1, question 3). Page numbers 155–185 indicate information found
    in Appendix A.

About the Authors _____

Patricia Younger, JD, Cynthia Conner, LL.L, and Kara Kinney Cartwright, JD, are Health Law Center staff members at Aspen Publishers, Inc., where they are involved in extensive research and writing on health law issues. Among the publications these attorneys write for are the *Hospital Law Manual,* a multivolume looseleaf treatise on a full range of health law issues, such as medical records, medical staff, pharmacy, consents, reproductive issues, tax, and financial management; the *Health Care Labor Manual,* a three-volume looseleaf treatise on labor and employment issues of concern to health care providers; and the *Managed Care Law Manual,* a treatise on legal issues of concern in the managed care environment, such as antitrust, utilization management, taxation, and fraud and abuse. In addition, these attorneys work with outside authors in producing the *Laboratory Regulation Manual,* a four-volume looseleaf treatise addressing legal issues of concern to clinical laboratories written by the law firm of O'Connor and Hannon; and the *Hospital Contracts Manual,* a three-volume treatise covering contracting issues relevant to health care providers, edited by the law firm of Baker and Hostetler.